Silence, Language, & Society

A guide to style and meaning,
grace and compassion

Silence
Language
& Society

A guide to style and meaning, grace and compassion

Robert Hartwell Fiske

Vocabula Books
Rockport, Massachusetts

Published by Vocabula Books, an imprint of Vocabula Communications Company, 5A Holbrook Court, Rockport, Massachusetts 01966.
First edition.

Some of the material in this book I have compiled from other books I have written. — RHF

ISBN: 978-0-9774368-7-3

Library of Congress Control Number: 2008928900

Read *The Vocabula Review* at www.vocabula.com

Vocabula Books
an imprint of
Vocabula Communications Company

A Gift For You

To: _____

From: _____

Date: _____

Contents

1. Silence, Language, and Society   10

| *Reflections on language and culture, thought
and sincerity*

2. What Matter Meaning?   39

| *Misspent words and the loss of meaning*

3. Oddments and Miscellanea   108

| *Responses and remarks, imprecations and polls*

Alas, where one man sees a goal — bright, beautiful, magnificent — another sees a gargoyle — ugly, repulsive, grotesque. Goal or gargoyle, magnificent or monstrous, still, let us not, at the end of our lives, have cause to curse the cowardliness with which we lived them.

Silence, Language, & Society

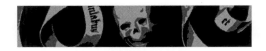

1. SILENCE, LANGUAGE, AND SOCIETY

1. Being silent is the chance to think, to talk to oneself, and it is preferable to much of what we say aloud. We need to speak, as we need to write, with more deliberation and clarity. Our sanity and our society depend on it. Thought is borne of quiet, of internal talk. In today's money-grubbing, entertainment-ridden, fear-induced society, there is scant value in being still and thinking for oneself.

2. Without the temperament to listen to our own thoughts and feelings, without the resolve to be silent and still, we will never make much of an impression on others. We will think as others think, and speak as others speak, but these, alone, are poor talents, barren of any true ability.

3. Be silent and all you neglected to consider, all you failed to feel, all you hoped to
say will unfold before you.

4. Let us have time to be silent and still,
time to reflect on the past and think about
the future; without it, no one is knowable.

5. About silence little can be said. Silence
soon succumbs to speech.

6. Even today — subjected as we are to the
apotheosis of popular culture — using the
English language respectfully helps us
maintain a sense of ourselves and our values. To do otherwise, to disregard the ways
of our words, is to forsake our humanity
and, perhaps, even forfeit our future.

7. Inadequate though they may be, words
distinguish us from all other living things.
Only we humans can reflect on the past
and plan for the future; it is language that
allows us to do so. Indeed, our worth is
partly in our words. Effective use of language — clear writing and speaking — is a
measure of our humanness.

8. The point of learning new words is not to
impress your friends or to seem more intel-

ligent than they. The point is to see more, to understand more. An ever-increasing vocabulary uncovers connections, introduces spheres, and — in reminding us that there are words for all thoughts, all feelings, all behaviors, all things — upholds all humankind.

9. The less well we use the language, the less thoughtful, cogent, and communicative we likely are.

10. When they do their work best, words help people communicate; they promote understanding between people. And this, being well understood, is precisely the goal we should all aspire to when writing and speaking. As obvious as this seems, it is not a goal we commonly achieve.

11. Words often ill serve their purpose. When they do their work badly, words militate against us. Poor grammar, sloppy syntax, abused words, misspelled words, and other infelicities of style impede communication and advance only misunderstanding.

12. We often believe that many words are better than few. Perhaps we imagine that the more we say, the more we know or the more others will think we know, or that the more obscure our writing is, the more profound our thoughts are. Seldom, of course, is this so. A superfluity of words conceals more than it reveals.

13. As never before, people do as others do, speak as others speak, and think as others think. The cliché is king. Nothing is so reviled as individuality. We imitate one another lest we be left alone. We want to fit in, to be part of the crowd. We want groups to engulf us and institutions to direct us.

14. Nothing turns a sentence so quickly as a cliché. The more of these sentences we read, the more our disposition sours and our disgust mounts.

15. Many of us seek to enhance our self-importance by using ostentatious language. We may believe that the more words we use, or the more elaborate our language, the more intelligent we sound and important we are. We may recognize the thinness of our thoughts and try to give them added weight by using polysyllabic words. Or we may chatter endlessly as though each word were further proof of our presence.

16. Some people through expedient, euphemistic, or circumlocutory language, strive to conceal their actions, to becloud what they say and do. With words they do whatever they please and, in so doing, manage to confuse our perception of their deeds and, even, their identity.

17. Academics and social scientists regularly try to give more prestige to their disciplines, and themselves, by breeding their own vocabularies.

18. Whereas people who aspire to write and speak the language well still maintain standards of speech and observe distinctions between words, the uneducated, like some juggernaut, massacre and obliterate. They slay nearly all that they say.

19. Much uneducated English is everyday English. The language pullulates with people who hover between the uneducated and the everyday.

20. Whereas a witticism is a clever remark or phrase — indeed, the height of expression — a "dimwitticism" is the converse; it is a commonplace remark or phrase. Dimwitticisms are worn-out words and phrases; they are expressions that dull our reason and dim our insight, formulas that we rely on when we are too lazy to express what we think or even to discover how we feel. The more we use them the more we conform — in thought and feeling — to everyone else who uses them.

21. Dimwitticisms are categorized by the following types:

• Grammatical gimmicks: Quite simply, *and everything* is a babbler's way of describing what he was unable to. This phrase and so many others like it — *and everything like that; and stuff (things); and (or) stuff (things) like that; and this and that; anyway; I mean; (and that) kind of stuff (thing); or something or other; or whatever; this, that, and the other (thing); you had to be there* — are grammatical gimmicks that we use to make up for the misfashioned words that precede them.

These are devices that we resort to whenever we are unable to explain adequately our thoughts or feelings. Grammatical gimmicks attest to just how dull and dimwitted we have become.

• Ineffectual phrases: Ineffectual phrases are the expressions people use to delay or obstruct, to bewilder or make weary. The intent of those who use ineffectual phrases is to make it appear as though their sentences are more substantial than they actually are, but not one sentence is made more meaningful by their inclusion: *(please) be advised that; I'll tell you (something); it has come to (my) attention; it is important to realize (that); it is interesting to note (that); make no mistake (about it); (to) take this opportunity (to); the fact of the matter is; the fact remains; the thing about it is; what happened (is).*

How a person speaks often reveals how he thinks. And how he thinks determines how he behaves. A person who speaks ineffectually may think ineffectually, and a person who thinks ineffectually may behave ineffectually — perhaps badly.

Ineffectual phrases add only to our being ineffectual people.

• Inescapable pairs: In an inescapable pair, the first word means much the same as the second or so often accompanies the second that any distinction between them is, in effect, forfeited.

Only occasionally, that is, do we see the word *allied* without the word *closely; asset* without *valuable; baby* without *beautiful; balance* without *delicate; distinction* without *dubious; error* without *egregious; tied* without *inextricably; missed* without *sorely; poverty* without *abject; principle* without *basic.*

And more often than not we find the word *aid* joined to *abet; alive* joined to *well; effective* joined to *efficient; hope* joined to *pray; hue* joined to *cry; pure* joined to *simple.*

When two words are treated as though they were one — the plight of every inescapable pair — our keenness is compromised, our discernment endangered.

No longer does every word tell; the words themselves have become witless.

• Infantile phrases: Any thought or feeling in which these expressions are found is likely to be made instantly laughable: *absolutely, positively; all of the above; because (that's why); because why?; (as) compared*

17

to what?; going on (19); I'll bet you any amount of money; in no way, shape, or form; intestinal fortitude; it takes one to know one; me, myself, and I; mission accomplished; mutual admiration society; never (not) in a million years; real, live; really and truly; (you) started it; (I) take it back; the feeling's mutual; the (L)-word; (my) whole, entire life; with a capital (A); (62) years young; (a) zillion(s) (of). Also included among these phrases that strike all but the dimwitted as derisory are notorious advertising slogans (*inquiring minds want to know; where's the beef*), song and film titles (*a funny thing happened to me on the way to; I can't get no satisfaction*), and alliterative or rhymed phrases (*a bevy of beauties; chrome dome*).

Other infantile phrases are more disturbing, for they reveal an adolescent, unformed reasoning. Explanations like *in the wrong place at the wrong time, it just happened, it's a free country,* and *everything's (it's all) relative* are as farcical as they are possibly fallacious.

• Moribund metaphors: Metaphors, like similes, should have the briefest of lives. Their vitality depends on their evanescence.

Yet must we ever endure the dimwitted *(it's)
a jungle (out there), an emotional roller
coaster, a stroll (walk) in the park, (like)
being run over (getting hit) by a (Mack) truck,
(as) cool as a cucumber, everything but the
kitchen sink, (as) hungry as a horse, leak
like a sieve, light at the end of the tunnel, out
to lunch, over the hill, pass like ships in the
night, (as) phony as a three-dollar bill, (a)
piece of cake, rule the roost, window of opportunity, (every parent's) worst nightmare,*
and countless other metaphors that char-
acterize people as dull, everyday speakers
and writers, indeed, as platitudinarians?
Nothing new do they tell us. Nothing more
do they show us.

Moreover, if it weren't for our plethora of
metaphors, especially, sports images —
*above par, a new ballgame, batting a thou-
sand, do (make) an end run around, down
for the count, hit a home run, off base, pull
no punches, stand on the sidelines, step up
to the plate, took the ball and ran with it —*
and war images — *a call to arms, an uphill
battle, battle lines are drawn, draw fire,
earn his stripes, first line of defense, in the
trenches, on the firing line, take by storm —*
men and, even, women would be far less
able to articulate their thoughts. We would

19

speak and write more haltingly than we already do; our thoughts and feelings more misshapen than they already are.

We rely on moribund metaphors not because we feel they make our speech and writing more vivid and inviting but because we fail to learn how to express ourselves otherwise; we know not the words.

In truth, the more of these metaphors we use, the less effective is our speech and writing. Neither interesting nor persuasive, their expression fatigues us where we thought it would inform us, annoys us where we believed it would amuse us, and benumbs us where we hoped it would inspire us.

• Overworked words: The broader your knowledge of words, the greater your ability to express yourself precisely and persuasively. Many speakers and writers, however, depend on certain words — overworked words like *action, actively, amazing, appreciate, approach, attitude, awesome, basically, crisis, definitely, devastate, effect, excellence, great, impact, implement, incredible, interesting, lasting, major, meaningful, mindset, natural, nice, ongoing, parameter, pretty, really, scenario, significant, situation, strange, thing, unbelievable, very, weird.*

Words, when overworked, diminish the meaning of all that they are used to describe. Our remarks and questions both are enfeebled by these tired terms. Nothing that we express with these overworked words has the force or effectiveness of less habitually spoken, less repeatedly written words. Moreover, since a person understands little more than what the words he is knowledgeable of convey — a word means only so much — to rely on so few words reveals just how limited a person's understanding of himself, and those about him, is.

Our knowledge of the world increases as our familiarity with words does.

• Plebeian sentiments: Plebeian sentiments reflect the views and values of the least thoughtful among us: *be nice; (I) gave (him) the best years of (my) life; (it) gives (me) something to do; (these things) happen to other people, not to (me); I (just) don't think about it; I just work here; I'm bored (he's boring); (it) keeps (me) busy; (it's) something to look forward to; there are no words to de-*

scribe (express); you think too much; what can you do; why me?

What's more, these expressions, base as they are, blunt our understanding and quash our creativity. They actually shield us from our thoughts and feelings, from any profound sense of ourselves.

People who use these expressions have not become who they were meant to be.

• Popular prescriptions: Powerless to repeat an author's epigram, unfit to recite a poet's verse, more than many of us are utterly able to echo a society's slogans and clichés: *absence makes the heart grow fonder; actions speak louder than words; a picture is worth a thousand words; beauty is in the eye of the beholder; better late than never; do as I say, not as I do; forgive and forget; hope for the best but expect the worst; it takes two; keep (your) nose to the grindstone; live and learn; misery loves company; money isn't everything; neither a borrower nor a lender be; take it one day (step) at a time; the best things in life are free; the meek shall inherit the earth; the sooner the better; time flies when you're having fun; two wrongs don't make a right; what goes around, comes around; you can't be all things to all people; you can't have everything.*

Popular prescriptions are the platitudes and proverbs by which people live their lives. It is these dicta that determine who we are and how we act; they define our intellectual and moral makeup.

Dull-witted speakers and writers depend on prescriptions like these to guide them through life. For this poor populace, life is, we may surmise, laid out. From the popular or proper course, there is scant deviation. Popular prescriptions endure not for their sincerity but for their simplicity. We embrace them because they make all they profess to explain and all they profess to prescribe seem plain and uncomplicated.

Inexorably, we become as simple as they — we people, we platitudes.

• Quack equations: *a deal is a deal; a politician is a politician; a promise is a promise; a rule is a rule; enough is enough; ethics is ethics; fair is fair; God is love; it is what it is; less is more; more is better; perception is reality; (what's) right is right; seeing is believ-*

*ing; talk is cheap; the law is the law is the
law; what happened happened; what's done
is done.* This is the sort of simplicity much
favored by mountebanks and pretenders,
by businesspeople and politicians. Quack
equations too readily explain behavior that
the undiscerning may otherwise find inex-
plicable and justify attitudes that they may
otherwise find unjustifiable. No remedies
for shoddy reasoning, no restoratives for
suspect thinking, these palliatives soothe
only our simple-mindedness.

Equally distressing is that there is no end
to these quack equations: *alcohol is alcohol;
he is who he is; math is math; money is
money is money; people are people; plastic is
plastic; prejudice is prejudice; their reasoning is their reasoning; the past is the past;
wrong is wrong.* Forever being fabricated
and continually being merchandized,
shoddy thinking is far more easily dis-
pensed than sound thinking.

• Suspect superlatives: In dimwitted usage,
superlatives are suspect. That which seems
most laudable is often least, that which
seems topmost, bottommost, that which
seems best, worst: *an amazing person; (I'm)
a perfectionist; area of expertise; celebrity;*

class; gentleman; great; personal friend; pursuit of excellence; the best and (the) brightest; the rich and famous.

• Torpid terms: Torpid terms are vapid words and phrases that we use in place of vital ones: *a majority of; a moving experience; a number of; a step (forward) in the right direction; cautiously optimistic; (take) corrective action; degree; effectuate; extent; (a) factor; incumbent upon; indicate; input; leaves a little (a lot; much; something) to be desired; move forward; negative feelings; off-putting; operative; prioritize; proactive; pursuant to; remedy the situation; represent(s); (the) same; send a message; shocked (surprised) and saddened (dismayed).*

Formulas as flat as these keep us dumb and dispassionate. They elicit the least from us.

With these unsound formulas, little can be communicated and still less can be accomplished. Torpid terms interfere with our understanding and with our taking action; they thwart our thinking and frustrate our feeling.

• Withered words: There are many rare and wonderful words that we would do well to become familiar with — words that would revitalize us for our revitalizing them — words like *bedizen; bootless; caliginous; compleat; cotquean; hebdomadal; helpmeet; logorrhea; quondam; wont.*

Withered words, however — words like *albeit; amidst; amongst; behoove; betwixt; ergo; forsooth; perchance; said; sans; save; thence; unbeknownst; verily; whence; wherein; whereon; wherewith; whilst* — are archaic and deserve only to be forgotten. People who use them say little that is memorable.

• Wretched redundancies: Reckless writers and slipshod speakers use many words where few would do: *advance planning; at this time; consensus of opinion; dead body; due to the fact that; first and foremost; free gift; just recently; in advance of; in and of itself; in spite of the fact that; in terms of; make a determination; on a ... basis; on the part of; past experience; period of time; (the) reason (why) is because; refer back; the single best (most); until such time as.* Yet for all the words, their expression is but impoverished; more words do not necessarily signify more meaning.

Life is measured by its meaning, and a good deal of that meaning is inherent in the words we use. If so many of our words are superfluous — and thus do not signify — so much of our life is, ineluctably, meaningless.

In the end, we are no more superfluous than are the words we use.

22. Each dimwitticism is a failure to write clearly and compellingly, an admission that the author could not manage an original thought or a better turn of phrase, or could not be bothered to think of one. Dimwitticisms yield only facile writing, only false sentiment.

23. Within sentences, among thoughts struggling to be expressed and ideas seeking to be understood, dimwitticisms ravage the writer's efforts as much as they do the reader's, the speaker's as much as the listener's.

24. People who rely on dimwitticisms appear to express themselves more fluently

and articulately than those few who do not.
But this is a sham articulateness, for without the use of phrases like *left holding the*
bag, left out in the cold, her worst nightmare,
and that type of stuff, basically, level the
playing field, stick out like a sore thumb, ar-
rive on the scene, shocked and saddened, it
is interesting to note, in the wrong place at
the wrong time, with a capital M, a breath of
fresh air, incredible, and *definitely,* most
people would stammer helplessly.

25. One of the difficulties with dimwitticisms is that, because they are so familiar,
people will most often use them thought-
lessly. Manacled as people are to these well-
worn phrases, original thoughts and fresh
words are often unreachable.

26. Dimwitticisms give rise to ineloquence,
and it is precisely this that marks so much
of our speech and writing. Whatever the occasion, whether celebratory or funereal,
quotidian or uncommon, people speak and
write the same dimwitted words and
phrases. No wonder so many of us feel barren or inconsolable: there are few words
that inspire us, few words that move us,
few words that thrill or overwhelm us. Per-

suasion has lost much of its sway, conviction, much of its claim.

27. Everyday language leads only to everyday thoughts and commonplace actions; few insights, fewer epiphanies, can be had with mediocre, with dimwitted, language.

28. Those of us who speak well are thought false and formal; the more articulate you are, the less approachable you are thought to be. It is not what you say that revolts others, but the structure, modest or monumental though it may be, of your sentences, the style, not the substance, of your speech.

The irony of this is as painful as it is patent. Speech, a predominantly, perhaps uniquely, human device, which is designed, as no other human means is, to help people communicate, to promote understanding between people, serves, when polished and precise, to make the speaker appear inaccessible. It is scarcely those who speak badly who hamper our language's capacity to communicate, it is we who speak well, who delight in style and subtleties of syntax rather than in jargon and gibberish.

As odious as this is, more odious still is that it signifies the exaltation of shoddiness. Soundness and sense have had their day; shoddiness now has the dais.

29. So prevalent is everyday English that the person who speaks correctly and uses words deliberately is often thought less well of than the person who speaks solecistically and uses slang unreservedly. Today, fluency is in disfavor. Neither everyday nor even uneducated English seems to offend people quite as much as does elegant English. People neither fume nor flinch when they hear ill-formed or senseless sentences. But let them listen to someone who speaks, or read someone who writes, elegantly, and they may be instantly repelled. Doubtless, well-turned phrases and orotund tones suggest to them a soul unslain.

30. As the superfluity of dimwitticisms makes plain, elegant English is English rarely heard, English seldom seen.

31. We all know far too well how to write everyday English, but few of us know how to write elegant English — English that is expressed with music as well as meaning, style as well as substance, grace as well as compassion.

32. The English language is wonderfully expressive and infinitely flexible. There are many thousands of words and many hundreds of ways in which to use them. We should celebrate its opulence and its elegance.

33. Elegant English is exhilarating; it stirs our thoughts and feelings as ably as dimwitted English blurs them.

34. It is not classism but clarity, not snobbery but sensibility that users of elegant English prize and wish to promote. Nothing so patently accessible as usage could ever be justly called invidious. As long as we recognize the categories of usage available to us, we can decide whether to speak and write the language well or badly. And we might more readily decide that elegant English is indeed vital were it more widely spoken by our public figures and more often written in our better books. Countless occasions where elegant English might have been used — indeed, ought to have been used — by a president or politician, a luminary or other notable, have passed with uninspired, if not bumbling, speech or writing.

35. A person who expresses himself with genuineness instead of in jargon, with feeling instead of in formulas, is capable as few have been, as few are, and as few will be; this is a person to heed.

36. The goal is to promote understanding and rouse people to action. The goal is to express ourselves as never before — in writing that demands to be read aloud, in speech that calls to be captured in print.

37. All it takes for a solecism to become standard English is people misusing or misspelling the word. And if enough people do so, lexicographers will enter the originally misused or misspelled word into their dictionaries, and descriptive linguists will embrace it as a further example of the evolution of English.

38. *Merriam-Webster's Collegiate Dictionary,* like other college dictionaries, actually promotes the misuse of the English language. Dictionaries are ever more a catalog of confusions, a list of illiteracies. Dictionaries acknowledge the errors that people make; by acknowledging them they, in effect, endorse them; by endorsing them, they are thought correct by the dull, duped public. Ultimately, all words will mean whatever we think they mean, indeed, whatever we want them to mean.

39. That a president can ask *Is our children learning?* a basketball star can use the word *conversate,* a well-known college professor can say *vociferous* when he means *voracious,* and another can scold a student for using the word *juggernaut* because she believes it means *jigaboo* is disturbing. But these are precisely the sorts of errors, if enough people make them, that the staff at Merriam-Webster will one day include in their dictionaries.

40. Over the last forty and more years, linguists and lexicographers have conspired to transform an indispensable reference work into an increasingly useless, increasingly dangerous one. Lexicographers are no longer harmless.

41. Dictionaries, today, do not necessarily tell us the correct meaning of words; they simply tell us how people use words — hardly a good measure of meaning.

42. Nothing dissuades a person quite so quickly from reading your writing as your having misused a word. Know the meanings of the words you use. Meaning, despite the meaninglessness, the idiocy, that engulfs us all, still matters.

43. The only meaning in life is what we assign to it. Similarly, we assign meaning to the principal way we express meaning, to our words. If we fail to observe the meaning of our words, we contribute to the meaninglessness of our lives.

44. Where meanings are mangled, minds are also.

45. Lexicographers are descriptivists, language liberals. The use of *disinterested* to mean *uninterested* does not displease a descriptivist. A prescriptivist, by contrast, is a language conservative, a person interested in maintaining standards and correctness in language use. To prescriptivists, *disinterested* in the sense of *uninterested* is the mark of uneducated people who do not know the distinction between the two words. And if there are enough uneducated people saying *disinterested* when they mean *uninterested* or *indifferent,* lexicographers enter the definition into their dictionaries. Indeed, the distinction between these words has all but vanished owing largely to irresponsible writers and boneless lexicographers.

46. If we ignore the distinctions between words, we begin to ignore or disapprove of the distinctions between people; individuality, which, even now, is not favorably regarded, will become increasingly frowned upon, eventually unlawful, perhaps.

47. Along with the evolution of language — the thousands of neologisms that new technologies and new thinking have brought about, for instance — there has been a concurrent, if perhaps less recognizable, devolution of language. The English language has become more precise for some users of it while becoming more plodding for others. Not a small part of this new cumbrousness is due to the loss of distinctions between words, the misuse of words, and other abuses of language.

48. Swear words are among the least expressive words available to us. They are boring and boorish at once. Using scatological phrases and swear words no longer shocks anyone and suggests only that you are not clever enough to think of better, more meaningful words. Very likely your writing is no more readable than you yourself are companionable.

49. Though sports and even the word *sports* may make us imagine action and excitement, sports metaphors are among the most prosaic expressions available to us. Those who use them are precisely as dull and uninspired as are their words.

50. As the meaning of one word distinguishes it from the meaning of another, so the words we use distinguish each of us from others. Language, how we express ourselves as much as what we express, is designed to discriminate; it distinguishes, it defines, it identifies. We choose our friends, we choose our work, and we choose our words.

51. Distinguish your writing and speaking from others', and you distinguish yourself.

52. Slang is ephemeral. A slang word popular one year may be forgotten the next. As clever as some slang is, if you use it in your writing, you'll ensure that your writing is equally ephemeral.

53. Since how a person speaks and writes is a fair reflection of how a person thinks and feels, shoddy language may imply a careless and inconsiderate people — a public whose ideals have been discarded and whose ideas have been distorted. And in a society of this sort, easiness and mediocrity are much esteemed.

54. Soon we will be a society unable to distinguish one word from another, sense from nonsense, truth from falsehood, good from evil. We will soon utter only mono- and di-syllabic words, be entertained only by what pleases our peers, and adore whatever is easy or effortless. Unfamiliar wording and original phrasing will soon sound incoherent or cacophonic to us, while well-known inanities like *have a nice day, what goes around comes around,* and *hope for the best but expect the worst* will serve as our mantras, our maxims, our mottoes.

55. No grace is found in jargon; no compassion in slang. Whenever we express stock sentiments and common vulgarisms, we surrender sincerity and forfeit honesty.

56. The more we ignore words and their meanings, grammar and its intent, the less we understand each other, and the less civil society.

57. The evidence is widespread, even inescapable, that society suffers if people use language sloppily. At the very least, people misunderstand — or may very well misunderstand — each other, which can result in anything from embarrassment to ruin.

58. Worse still is the deliberate misuse of language. We all have suffered from the euphemisms, the circumlocutions, and the unadorned duplicity of businesspeople, politicians, lawyers, and others. With each word of deceit, something is undone: truth and meaning, grace and compassion, society itself.

59. More than incorrect grammar and an infelicitous style, the deliberate misuse of words is an assault on language and society.

60. A society is generally as lax as its language.

2. WHAT MATTER MEANING?

abberation *Abberation* is how aberrant users of the English language spell *aberration*. The language has its deviants, its descriptive linguists, its dictionary makers.

a (welcome) breath of fresh air Of what it purports to describe, *a (welcome) breath of fresh air* offers the opposite. If intelligent or heartfelt sentences are invigorating, this dimwitticism should make us gasp as though we've been throttled by foul-smelling thoughtlessness.

accidently At least two well-known dictionaries do recognize the spelling *accidently*. But let this be a further reminder that dictionaries merely record how people use the language, not necessarily how it ought to be used. Some dictionaries, we can reasonably infer, actually promote illiteracy. If we were to rely exclusively on dictionary pronouncements, we'd be altogether un-done.

actively The popular use of *actively* suggests that any verb not affixed to it is feckless. We cannot simply *consider* an idea lest we be accused of not thinking; we cannot simply *engage* in a pursuit lest we be accused of not trying; we cannot simply *participate* in a conversation lest we be accused of not speaking.

• Another possibility is *actively being considered* by the administration: the use of force.
• Brother David, a successful lawyer, refers clients but doesn't *actively engage in* sleuthing.
• After talking to many people who *actively participate* on the site, I'm confident that a year from now Mixx will be a force to be reckoned with.

adjectify As not every phrase can be reduced to a single word, so not every noun should be made into a verb. *Adjectify* — which apparently means to use as an adjective — sounds dreadful, and its meaning is questionable in nearly every context. If meaning it must have, *adjectify* should

mean to modify; to qualify, limit, or specify
the meaning of. *Adjectify,* at least in some
instances, seems to mean to describe or define. And *adjectify,* to the allusive ear,
sounds as though it means to dehumanize
or objectify.

A few words whose meaning is apparent are
better than one word whose meaning is not.

affidavid More than a misspelling,
affidavid signals that ineptitude and ignorance overwhelm us; today, entertainment
is all; learning how to spell correctly or
write well interests us no more than do civility and justice, honesty and integrity, yet
how we use language is inseparable from
how we view and participate in the world.

(for) a laugh This expression is spoken by
people who tally their giggles and count
their guffaws, people who value numbers
and sums more than they do words and
concepts, people who consider laughter a
commodity and life a comedy.

alive and kicking One of the conse-
quences of endlessly saying and hearing
and writing and reading formulaic phrases

is that, eventually, people *do* become weary of them.

But instead of expressing themselves differently — more eloquently or more inventively, perhaps — people will simply substitute one word in these selfsame formulas for another.

Thus, along with *alive and kicking,* there is, for instance, *alive and well* and even *alive and thriving;* along with *a thing of the past,* there is *a phenomenon of the past;* along with *business as usual,* there is *politics as usual* and *life as usual;* along with *mover and shaker,* there is *mover and shaper;* along with *neck of the woods,* there is the noisome *portion of the earth;* along with *needs and wants,* there is *needs and desires;* along with *in no way,* there is *in no way, shape, or form* and the preposterous *in no way, shape, form, or fashion;* along with *remedy the situation,* there is *rectify the situation;* along with *out the window,* there is *out the door;* and along with *nothing could be further from the truth,* there is, incomprehensibly, *nothing could be further from the actual facts.*

Would that it ended here, but there are also far too many people who begin with a hackneyed phrase and then transmogrify it into an ever-so-silly, garish one.

Thus, *between a rock and a hard place* becomes: • In the past decade, newspaper publishers have felt squeezed *between the Net and a hard place.* • The Al Queda fighters are *between an anvil and a hammer.*

A needle in a haystack becomes: • Her friend wrote back and said this was impossible, like looking for *a needle on the bottom of the ocean.*

From bad to worse becomes: • Moscow now has about 90 days to try to keep a *bad situation from collapsing into something infinitely worse.*

Doesn't have a snowball's chance in hell becomes: • There is nobody on Russia's political horizon who embraces Mr. Yeltsin's westernized brand of economic policy and *has a Siberian snowball's chance of winning a presidential election.*

An accident waiting to happen becomes:

• The holidays are *a cornucopia of awkward moments waiting to happen.* • Expectations are *resentments waiting to happen.*

Not with a bang but with a whimper becomes: • This week *started out with a bang and ended with a whimper* for bank stocks. • Hurricane Bonnie hit New England *with a whimper, not a bang.* • After *beginning my career there with a bang, I cannot end with a whimper.* • It could *end with a whimper or a wallop.*

Walk softly and carry a big stick becomes: • The guiding principle in foreign policy of this administration seems to be *speak loudly and carry a twig.*

Light at the end of the tunnel becomes: • Is it possible that we're actually seeing a *light at the end of Star Trek's TV continuum?*

Not worth the paper it's written (printed) on becomes: • Consumers can put their trust in a few of these Web site seals, but in many cases they *aren't worth the pixels that they're painted with.*

Going to hell in a hand basket becomes:

• The good news, culturally speaking, is that if we're *going to Hell in a Saks shopping bag,* at least we are going there slowly.

People propagate these monstrosities. Equally distressing is that, in doing so, they think they *are* being clever and inventive. Among pedestrian people, this is what it means to be thoughtful, this is what it means to be creative.

Is it any wonder that speech is so often soporific, writing so often wearisome?

alleve   A mix of *relieve* and *alleviate,* and a dose of the medication Aleve, the nonword *alleve* is being used by people who have more familiarity with television commercials than they do with written literature. This is as laughable as it is appalling.

a living hell   The force and colorfulness of this metaphor is no longer evident. An uncommonly used word — such as *chthonic, insupportable, plutonic, sulfurous, stygian,* or *tartarean* — is often more potent and captivating than a commonly used metaphor.

(take) a look see This phrase is one of the new illiteracies. Expressions like *a good read, a must have,* and *a look see* are favored today by the "illiterati" — smart, articulate people who find it fashionable to speak unintelligibly.

alterate Some people have a fondness for adding suffixes like *-ate* or *-ity* or *-ster* to words they either don't know the correct forms of or hope to add some small weight to. *Alterate* is not a word; *alter* is.

alternate If some people insist on maintaining the distinctions between *alternate* and *alternative,* it's because they prefer clarity to confusion, elegance to license.

ambivalent The meanings of *ambivalent* and *ambiguous* are decidedly different. Let us not waste the words we have under the false rubric, the artificial idealism, of liberalism or democracy, which as espoused by some, asserts one word may mean much the same as another. Neglecting or not knowing the distinctions between words can lead only to ambiguity and ambivalence at best, anarchy and turmoil at worst.

an accident waiting to happen *An accident waiting to happen* twists seriousness into silliness. The significance of what we say, the danger, perhaps, in what we do, we seldom see when we think with such frivolous phrases. Our understanding may be distorted, our responses dulled.

an amazing person *An amazing person* is so only in the eyes of another who, we can be confident, is not.

(it's) a nightmare How impoverished our imaginations are. Nightmares ought to be terrifying, but this metaphor — so popular has it become — is hopelessly tame. *It was a nightmare* instills in us as little compassion as it does interest; it makes us yawn rather than yell. No longer is there terror to it.

Altogether remarkable about this expression is that people use it to describe something that tormented or terrified them. They describe an extraordinary event with an ordinary phrase. How can we not doubt the sincerity of their words, the terror of their experience? Is this then what it is to be human — using platitudes to express what affects us most deeply?

annoyment *Annoyment,* an archaic varia-
tion of *annoyance,* has no place in today's
English language usage where words for
being annoyed are already superabundant.

appreciate You can *appreciate* an attribute
or occurrence ("I appreciate her thoughtfulness"; "I appreciate your coming"), but not
a person ("I appreciate you"; "I appreciate
so many folks enduring the rain"). Using
appreciate in the sense discouraged here is
the mark of people who have no notion of
eloquence and style, scant appreciation of
the limits of language, and little insight into
themselves or their audience.

(take) appropriate (corrective) action
This ponderousness phrase will stem one
person's drive while it saps another's de-
sire. From such a phrase, only dull-minded
deeds and uninspired acts may result,
which is quite likely all that the user of it,
bureaucrat he routinely is, either wishes for
or can imagine.

architect To *architect* is an absurdity. Not
everyone can concoct an effervescent verb
from some stolid noun. Though nouns do
indeed occasionally become verbs, *architect*
is hardly a good candidate, for many other

words already provide the definitions, and more exacting ones at that. A word not born of need begets only noise.

a (good) read This is a hideous expression that only the very badly read — those, that is, who read merely to be entertained — could possibly verbalize. The people who use this phrase are the people who read best-selling authors.

Read as a noun is one of the shibboleths by which people who care about language identify people who do not. Today there are people who try to speak and write well, and there are people who have no such aspiration.

(like) a (an emotional) roller-coaster (ride) Without relentless amusement, endless diversions, people might manage to speak tolerably well. As it is, the need to be entertained so overcomes us that we can speak in little but laughable images. The expression *(like) a (an emotional) roller-coaster (ride),* one such image, results from and gives rise to only carnival-like conversation, sideshow prose.

assertation *Assertation,* a thoroughly obsolete word used by fearfully modern people, is incorrect for *assertion. Assertation* — like the equally preposterous *documentate* (instead of *document*) and *opinionation* (instead of *opinion*) — is spoken or written by people who do not know the words they use, by people who do not read, by people who believe adding a syllable or two to a word ought not to affect its meaning: humanity lies elsewhere.

as the saying goes (is) This phrase reminds us of our ordinariness. *As the saying goes (is)* announces our having spoken, and thought, words that countless others have spoken and thought. What thoughts are we missing, what images are unavailable to us because we use the same damn words and phrases again and again? Let us strive for better than banality.

at the end of the day This overworked expression has superseded the equally silly *in the final (or last) analysis.* More sensible phrases include *eventually, finally, in the end, in time, ultimately*, but people, unsure of who they are, and concerned largely with comfort, imitate one another; people today say *at the end of the day.* If we were less inclined to say what others say (and do what others do), the world might be a wholly different place. Reason might even prevail.

avid reader An *avid reader* suggests someone who reads little more than mysteries, romance novels, and self-help books. These are people whose avidity is more for how many books they read than it is for any true meaning in books — people, that is, who prefer counting to reading.

awesome *Awesome* ought to be used to mean inspiring awe, fear, or admiration; extremely impressive or intimidating. In the informal sense of excellent, it is a very poor choice of words indeed. More than that, people who use *awesome* to mean excellent are, in fact, describing something that is, to keener minds, invariably mediocre or mindless, ridiculous or even repugnant.

basically People often use *basically* thinking it lends an intellectual air to the meaning of their words. *Basically,* in truth, only steals the sense from whatever words accompany it, for it proclaims their uncertainty and inexactitude as loudly as it does the speaker's or writer's pomposity.

Of course, there are also people, with few pretensions, who use *basically* either because they do not know what they say or because they do not know what to say.

be nice "Be nice," we often are admonished. There can be no complaint with being agreeable when agreeability is warranted, but to soporiferously accept niceness as a virtue, untarnished and true, is utterly benighted. To be capable of expressing anger and indignation is thwarted by our society's placing a premium on politeness. Let us not, of course, be rude gratuitously, nor seek to be singular for its own sake, nor foolish or fantastic for the quick cachet. Do, however, let us become more concerned with giving fuller expression to ourselves.

We do possibly irreparable harm to ourselves when, to avoid unpleasantness, we fail to show another how we truly feel. Unknown to ourselves and unknowable to others we homunculi are, for anonymity is won when anger is lost.

best-selling author *Best-selling authors,* of course, are responsible for the worst written books.

braggadocious Though the noun *brag-gadocio* (a braggart) is a word, the adjective *braggadocious* is not. Let us admire those who use the word *braggadocio,* and mock those who use *braggadocious.*

cachet *Cachet* (kah-SHAY) is a mark that indicates something is authentic, or superior; a distinction; a seal on a document; a commemorative design on an envelope; a medicinal wafer or capsule. *Cache* (KASH) is a hiding place for storing supplies, weapons, valuables, or other items; the items stored.

Because few people know the meaning of these two words, and fewer still the difference in their pronunciations, we can be sure that dictionaries will soon offer (KASH) as a variant pronunciation of *cachet,* and (kah-SHAY) as a variant of *cache.* Dictionaries: the new doomsday books.

cautiously (guardedly) optimistic *Optimistic* is a perfectly vigorous word, but modified by *cautiously* or *guardedly,* as it so often is, it becomes valueless. *Cautiously optimistic* is a phrase favored by poltroons and politicians, most of whom make a point of devaluing the meaning of their words.

celebrity As the most popular books are sometimes the least worthy of being read, so the most public people are sometimes the least worthy of being known.

If we must acknowledge these creatures — these *celebrities* — let us better understand them for who they are. All dictionary definitions of *celebrity* should include: 1. a mediocrity; a vulgarian; a coxcomb. 2. a scantly talented person who through shameless self-aggrandizement and utter inanity becomes widely known. 3. a repellent person.

class The antithesis of culture, *class* is a quality possessed by those who have neither elegance nor grace nor poise nor polish.

clean Evidence that some people — marketers and advertisers more than most — have contempt for their audiences is their using the abomination *clean.* Some words are to be cherished, some to be questioned, and some, like the noun *clean* — and whoever uses it — to be disdained.

collaborate Whereas *collaborate* means to work together to accomplish something, *corroborate* means to confirm the truth of something. If people fail to enunciate their words, if they do not distinguish their liquid *l*s from their liquid *r*s, dictionary makers will one day dictate that these two words sound alike and mean the same.

columnize Whatever is the point of *columnize*? Will we soon also have to endure *paragraphize* and *articleize*? Columnists write columns, articles; only the least able, or the most Corinthian, of them would say *columnize* instead of *write*.

commoditize *Commodify* means to turn into or treat as a commodity — which is also what *commoditize* is meant to mean. In other words, *commoditize* is likely a word born of error and ignorance, perhaps of people mispronouncing *commodify*. This is not, as descriptive linguists might maintain, an example of the evolution of English; it's an example of its devolution, its — when one word isn't distinguished from another (in this instance, a good word from a bad one) — commodification (*not,* commoditization). And the commodification of the language can result only in the commodification of the people who use the language.

compassionated Though *compassionated,* in the sense of pitied or sympathized with, was used by Mary Wollstonecraft Shelly, Anne Brontë, Charles Dickens, Sinclair Lewis, Frederick Douglass, Herman Melville, Abraham Lincoln, and others in the past, it is not used today, in the sense of compassionate — except by people who do not read Shelly, Brontë, Dickens, Lewis, Douglass, Melville, Lincoln.

conversate Over the last few years, this ridiculous word has cleaved to young adults, sports figures, and, now, others equally ill advised. Any dictionary that eventually adds this word born of imbecility to its pages is a dictionary to be disdained. As it is, we ought to consider whether we can gainfully consult a dictionary that includes the comical, the infantile *humongous.*

(I) could (should) write a book If all those who proclaim *I could write a book* — or all those who are advised *You should write a book* — were to do so, we would be immersed (more than we already are) in the vengeful, petty, or everyday lamentations of hollow-headed homemakers, shameless celebrities, and failed or forgotten business-people.

debark You might *debark* logs or trees, or, others, despicably, dogs, but you never *debark* or *disbark* a plane, train, or boat. Some people, apparently, cannot be bothered to pronounce polysyllabic words like *disembark*.

debone As *shell* means to remove the shell from, so *bone* means to remove the bones from. Because people, for decades, have mistakenly used *debone* to mean to remove the bones from, most dictionaries now include this definition with no qualifying remarks — further evidence that the word *dictionary* will, before long, mean rubbish; rot; claptrap; tripe; offal.

degree *Degree,* like *extent* — and the superfluity of phrases in which it is found — should be excised from almost all of our speech and writing. No sentence is made more compelling by the use of this word and its diffuse phrases.

• I believe he has *a very high degree* of integrity and takes extreme pride in his workmanship.

• Increased employee morale would require *a lesser degree* of accuracy.
• In some cases, they've been transformed *to such an extent* that you can no longer recognize them.
• The study said that women, *to a greater extent* than men, manage by personal interactions with their subordinates.

These are lifeless expressions, and it is listless people who use them.

devastate We can hardly wonder why so many of us are so easily *devastated.* This word is pervasive. Rarely are we *disconsolate, flustered,* or *unnerved.* If only we would use more measured terms, we might feel less weak and woundable.

dis Haven't we all had quite enough of this prefix aspiring to be a word? Are we to allow *un* and *anti, non* and *pre* to follow? People are increasingly mono- and disyllabic as it is; let's rail against this foolishness, this affront, this *dis.*

If you speak in monosyllables, you likely think in monosyllables. Complex thoughts, well-reasoned arguments, a keen understanding all then are lost.

discrimitory The fast-paced occasionally mispronounce *discriminatory,* and the slow-minded often misspell it.

disinterest *Disinterest* means without bias or impartial; it does not now mean uninterest or indifference. To use *disinterest* in the sense of uninterest is to forsake the word itself and, in effect, is a diminution of the foremost way in which we maintain our humanity: using language effectively.

disprefer Among linguists and their lackeys, disaffected as they often are from sense and thoughtfulness, *disprefer* actually does exist. No sentence is improved, none made true or clear, by using *disprefer* instead of some other wording.

• They will *disprefer* tentative expressions, such as hedges like possibly.
• Stoics rationally *disprefer* poverty (as an example) both for themselves and for other people.

downtalk One word or two, *downtalk* is as much as some people can manage. Words like *vilify* and *denigrate, malign* and *defame* may be unknown or misused by people who know and use baby talk.

due to circumstances beyond (our) control Of those who use this phrase, we may remark that their speech is no more grammatical than their actions are genuine. *Due to,* as often as not, should be *because of* or *owing to,* and only the similarly disingenuous would believe that *circumstances beyond our control* is an explanation rather than an evasion.

In the end, those who express themselves badly are less credible than those who express themselves well.

effective and efficient Businesspeople, in particular, seem unable to use the word *effective* without also using *efficient.* And though businesses endlessly plume themselves on how *effective and efficient* they are (and how excellent their products and services are), this is rarely true. The dimwitted *effective and efficient* more accurately means: 1. shoddy and inept. 2. uncaring and purblind. 3. money-grubbing and malevolent.

enormacy There are two words: *enormousness,* which means outstandingly big or huge, and *enormity,* which means monstrously evil or wicked. *Enormacy,* an arrangement of letters that some people may think encompasses both outstandingly big and monstrously evil, is no word and has no meaning.

enthuse *Enthuse,* a malformation capable only of misshaping whatever sentence it appears in, is one of those words that reveal more than its users may suppose. Aside from expressing its irregular meaning, *enthuse* exposes its users as slapdash speakers and indifferent writers.

envisualize We have *visualize* and *envision,* but not *envisualize.* Linguists call this a "lexical blend"; the rest of us call it what it truly is: nonsense.

et cetera (etc., etc.; et cetera, et cetera) When thoughts stumble and then stop, words, or at least intelligible words, do as well. As often as not, *et cetera* is a means of expressing, without having to admit to their meaning, all those words only dimly thought.

every effort is being made This phrase, disembodied though it is, serves to disarm people as it dismisses them.

excellence The word is overworked and the concept undervalued. Too much, today, passes for *excellence*. Too much of our work is shoddy, too much of our wisdom, suspect, too much of our worth, unsure.

extremify In using *extremify,* people acknowledge their inability to think well. We use incorrect words, counterfeit words, simple assemblages when we cannot think of the better built words available to us.

extrenuating No one who reads, or who reads carefully, could possibly say or write *extrenuating.* Instead of judging one another by how much money we earn or by how big our house is, let us judge one another by more telling talents: by whether and how well we read.

fashion statement Making a *fashion statement* is the concern of adolescents and addle-brained adults who have yet to fashion for themselves a sense of identity. Their habiliments interest them more than does their humanity.

People so intent on being fashionable make only misstatements. They but blither.

fateful *Fatal* means resulting in death; disastrous. *Fateful* means determined by fate; prophetic; significant. Several dictionaries maintain that *fatal* also means *fateful,* but the true meaning of this is that dictionaries are as unreliable as they are unreadable.

fearful Though many dictionaries declare that *fearful* and *fearsome* are synonyms, dictionaries — it must be remembered — merely record how people use the language. It is far better to use *fearful* to mean afraid or frightened, and *fearsome* to mean causing fear. If we allow one word to mean much the same as another, we have fewer words that matter. If we have fewer words, nuance and knowledge are lost.

first (highest; number-one; top) priority Nothing soulful can be said using these expressions, so when a U.S. cardinal drearily sermonizes "The protection of children must be our *number-one priority,*" we are hardly convinced that this is his or the church's principal concern. When we read, in some corporate promotional piece, "Your satisfaction is our *number-one priority,*" we are likewise, and for good reason, suspicious. Mechanical expressions like *first (highest; number-one; top) priority* defy tenderness, resist compassion, and counter concern.

friend • That said, if you've read this and agree, do *friend* me. • Did they *friend* you or did you *friend* them? • I *friend* people for a variety of reasons; some *friend* me back, some don't. To *friend* is being used instead of *befriend* or, perhaps, *ask to be my friend.*

In some ways, the verb *friend* corresponds to the verb *fuck*: "do fuck me ...," "did they fuck you ... did you fuck them?" "I fuck people ... some fuck me back." Monosyllabic labiodentals both, *fuck* and *friend* are different only in that *fuck,* in the sense of "to make love," is a powerful, meaningful word, whereas *friend,* in the sense of "to befriend," has no more power or meaning than every other sense of *fuck.*

gift Though *gift* as a verb is an antiquated form, the use of it today is nonsense, even offensive. When we have words like *give* and *donate* or *make a gift of, gift* the verb is patent commercialese for *buy* or *purchase.* To *gift* is meant to encourage us to *buy.*

ginormous Combining *gigantic* and *enormous, ginormous* is a word for which we already have a great many synonyms. It's easy to create synonyms of readily understandable concepts like largeness.

Better than new, ill-defined words for simple concepts like largeness would be new words for less easily understood or less often encountered concepts like bravery or justice or truth. Having more synonyms of words such as these may, over time, affect people's behavior and increase the occurrence of bravery, the spread of justice, or the value of truth.

Ginormous is a silly slang term that does nothing to improve our understanding of ourselves or our world. What's more, some people, simple though the concept of large should be, apparently have trouble understanding the word:

• It was a *ginormous* year for the wordsmiths at Merriam-Webster.
• She gave her mom, Kathy, a *ginormous* hug before the hotel entrepreneurs sped off to their Bel-Air mansion for some quality time together.
• But I have one *ginormous* point to add.

go forward, move forward Only the least eloquent speakers use *go forward* or *move forward in the right direction*. These expressions, and others like them, are wholly unable to move us. Inefficacious all, they dull our minds and immobilize our actions.

These useless expressions are spoken and written by people who seem unable to remember that the English language has both a present and a future tense. *Going forward, moving forward,* and the like are used instead of, or along with, present- or future-tense expressions. This may mean that, before long, people will not easily be able to distinguish between the present and the future, or that they may not be able to think in terms of the future. Already, there is evidence of this, for many of us are without imagination and foresight.

great *Great* is a suspect superlative, for that which is called *great* is seldom more than *good,* and that which is *good* is scarcely mentionable. *Great expectations* often turn out to be slight realizations, and *great stuff* is seldom more than stuff.

green light Like *red light,* the expression *green light* appeals to people who grasp the meaning of colorful visuals and expressive pictures more easily than they do polysyllabic words and complicated thoughts. Some people upgrade simple or straightforward ideas to unintelligible ones; others degrade substantive or nuanced ideas to unsophisticated ones. *Green light* is an example of the latter, but both tactics suggest an insincere mind, an unknowable heart.

have a good (nice) day (evening) We are bovine creatures who find that formulas rather than feelings suit us well enough; indeed, they suit us mightily. How pleasant it is not to have to think of a valid sentiment when a vapid one does so nicely; how effortless to rely on triteness rather than on truth. Dimwitticisms veil our true feelings and avert our real thoughts.

have (take) a listen As inane as it is insulting, *have (take) a listen* obviously says nothing that *listen* alone does not. Journalists and media personalities who use this offensive phrase ought to keep still.

heartship This misusage further signals the future of the English language. If people continue to heed laxicographers and descriptive linguists (fascinated as they are by this kind of "new usage"), the words will not matter. "Any spelling, any usage, any meaning" — the motto of all ding-a-linguists.

hecticity This is an abominable word — one that a silly celebrity or a descriptive linguist might love. As you see, many words readily mean what *hecticity* struggles to. That this word is used by a few impressionable people is hardly reason for more discriminating ones to embrace it. Not all words are worthy.

• By now I am accustomed to all the *hecticity* of these events.
• Since the concept of alienation is too wide and varied, I refined my goal by concentrating on the *hecticity* of contemporary urban life.
• Amid the *hecticity* of existence, we perceive the celestial bodies as phenomena that calm and reassure.

hero Seldom someone who strives valorously to achieve a noble goal, *hero* has come to mean anyone who simply does his job or, perhaps, doing it, dies. As often, *hero* is used to describe a person who behaves ethically or suitably — merely, as he was told or taught. Only comic book characters and cartoon creatures, today, define the word well.

Heroes are also common people who are uncommonly aware of how they use the language. They speak and write with care and deliberation. They are the people who, despite weak-willed lexicographers, descriptive linguists, peer-fearful adolescents, and others as pitiable, know the distinctions between words and observe them.

hey As a substitute for *hello* or *hi, hey* is a cheerless one. Perhaps the best way to discourage people from using *hey* is to respond with a hearty *diddle, diddle?*

Certain words do not belong to the realm of writing, or at least nonfiction writing: *hey* is clearly one of them. *Hey* is exclamatory, but only less than able writers — however friendly they wish to appear — would use it, in effect, as an inverted exclamation mark with which to capture our flagging attention.

how goes it? (how's it going? how you doing?) These phrases are uttered by the unalert and inert. *How goes it? how's it* *going?* and *how you doing?* are gratuitous substitutes for a gracious *hello.* Genuine expressions of courtesy such as *please* and *thank you* and *you're welcome* have been usurped by glib ones such as *have a nice day* and *I appreciate it* and *no problem.*

The worsening of our speech accompanies the withering of our souls.

humongous Not quite a misusage, *humongous* is altogether a monstrosity. It is a hideous, ugly word. And though it's not fair to say that people who use the word are hideous and ugly as well, at some point we come to be — or at the least are known by — what we say, what we write.

I can't believe I'm telling you this Only the foolish or the unconscious, unaware of or ambivalent about the words they use or why they use them, can exclaim *I can't believe I'm telling you this.* Language use, the essence of being human, entails certain responsibilities — care and consciousness among them; otherwise, it's all dimwitted.

I don't know For a person to conclude his expressed thoughts and views with *I don't know* would nullify all he seemed to know if

it weren't that *I don't know* is less an admission of not knowing than it is an apol-
ogy for presuming to.

• New passion is sweet, but after you
know someone for a while, it fades. *I don't
know.*
• I know who I am — I have a good sense of
that — but I will never know you, or anyone
else, as well. *I don't know.*

I feel (understand) your pain The people
who spout about how empathic they are (*I
feel your pain; I know how you feel*) are
often the same people who have scant notion of what it is to be sensitive, kind-
hearted, even responsive. The emphasis is
on showing empathy, which we do more for
our own welfare than for others'; it's socially obligatory to be, or pretend to be, empathic. Ultimately, empathy will be thought
no more highly of than sympathy now is.

I'll tell you (something) Like *I'll tell you
what, I'm telling you, let me tell you (something),* and *I (I've) got to (have to) tell you
(something), I'll tell you (something)* is
mouthed by unimpressive men and irritat-
ing women. These are mind-numbing expressions spoken by people who are largely

71

unaware of what they say. Few expressions define a person as quickly as these.

A phrase rarely written is a phrase that should be seldom spoken.

I love (him) but I'm not in love with (him) The need to distinguish between loving someone and being *in* love with someone is fundamentally false. That there are different kinds of love is nothing that any discerning person has to be reminded of.

Some who make such a distinction may do so to ease their conscience, to absolve themselves for not loving someone who likely loves them and whom they surely feel gratitude or obligation to. In these instances, saying *I love (him) but I'm not in love with (him)* is simply a way of feeling good about having made someone feel bad.

Love, like few other words, ought not to be trifled with.

I'm bored (he's boring) Being boring is preferable to being bored. The boring are often thoughtful and imaginative; the bored, thoughtless and unimaginative.

We would do well to shun those who whine about how bored they are or how boring another is. It's they, these bored ones, who in their eternal quest for entertainment and self-oblivion are most suited to causing trouble, courting turmoil, and coercing talk.

I mean   Elliptical for "what I mean to say," *I mean* is said by those who do not altogether know what they mean to say.

imply   To *imply* is to suggest; to *infer* is to conclude. Speakers and writers imply; listeners and readers infer. Some dictionaries, continuing their disservice to us all, consider these two words synonymic, defining one with the other. The first thing we do, let's kick all the laxicographers.

in any way, shape, form, or fashion   That anyone uses this expression is wondrous. To discerning people, *in any way, shape, form, or fashion,* as well as similar assemblages, is as rickety as it is ridiculous.

incent   *Incentivize* instead of *motivate* or *encourage* is quite bad enough, but *incent* instead of *incentivize* is execrable, as laughable as it is idiotic. What's more, *incent* reveals how unspeakable — how difficult to say — *incentivize* is to the people, the businesspeople largely, in whose vocabulary it is.

inclimate If laxicographers continue to compile dictionaries, *inclimate* will soon be listed as a variant spelling of *inclement.* Should that happen, burn their books.

infusement The word is *infusion,* the introduction of a new element or quality into something. *Infusement* means nothing at all — though, to those who say nothing at all, it might indeed mean something.

intrepity To misspell or mispronounce *intrepidity* as *intrepity* (in-TREP-i-tee) may diminish the courage and mock the fearlessness of whomever the word is used to describe; it certainly diminishes and mocks the person misusing the word.

Observing the correct spelling, pronunciation, and meaning of words is among our most important obligations. Ignore this, and people will likely ignore you.

issueization *Issueization* (or *issuization*), like *issueize* (or *issuize*), is apparently meant to mean turning (something) into an issue, a problem, concern, or worry. Occasionally, it may also mean issuance or issuing, though in many instances, it's not altogether clear what the word is meant to mean — a very good reason not to use it.

it doesn't take (you don't have to be) a rocket scientist (an Einstein; a PhD) to (know) We can be reasonably certain that the people who use this expression are not rocket scientists, not Einsteins, not PhDs. We can be less certain that the people who use this phrase are not dull-witted, not obtuse, not brainless.

it just happened As an explanation for how circumstances or incidents unfold, none is more puerile. And though we might excuse children such a sentiment, it is rarely they who express it. *It just happened* is a phrase used by those too slothful or too fearful to know what has happened.

it's a long story *It's a long story* — cipher for "I don't want to tell you" — is a mannerly expression that we use to thwart the interest of a person in whom we are not much interested.

it's not over till (until) it's over People say *it's not over till (until) it's over* in earnest, as if it were a weighty remark, a solemn truth when, of course, it's nothing but dimwitted. We might have an occasional insight, even a revelation, if we didn't persistently speak, and think, this kind of rubbish.

(the) jury is still out Still another way to express not knowing or being undecided, *the jury is still out,* used figuratively, is as foolish a phrase as it is a meaning.

Any sentence in which this dimwitticism is used is sentenced to being forgettable.

keep smiling *Keep smiling* is insisted on by ghoulish brutes who would rob us of our gravity, indeed, steal us from ourselves.

laconic The meaning of the word *laconic* is terse, concise; using few words. It does not mean unemotional, affectless, or dispassionate.

When a word takes on a new meaning — often a wholly incorrect and inappropriate meaning — laxicographers and linguists, bungling, clumsy arbiters of the language, call it a "semantic shift" or "semantic drift." More sensible people call it idiocy.

laxadaisical Though some people might, on occasion, allow, even applaud, the spelling *laxicographer* (a hopelessly descriptive dictionary maker), no one should allow the misspelling *laxadaisical*.

learnings *Learning* no one can find fault with, but *learnings* is a different word, and a ridiculous one. *Learning* has been made plural so as to include the meanings of a dozen other words, more precise words. People are impatient with, even intolerant of, exactitude and nicety. We are no more careful of our words than we are caring for one another. The less exact our words, the less clear our thoughts, the less sincere our sentences, the less honest our behavior.

less The distinction between *fewer* and *less* (like that between *number* and *amount*) centers on what can be counted and what cannot. *Fewer* we use for numbers; *less* we use for quantities.

Even the confusion between these two words is being sanctioned by lexicographers, for many dictionaries now offer one word as the synonym of the other. In the end, lexicographers who suppress or discourage the distinctions between words reduce our ability to see clearly and reason convincingly.

let me tell you something Of course the people who use this phrase seldom enunciate *let me;* they mutter *lemme,* an inauspicious sign, we might reasonably believe, of what is to come. *Let me tell you (something)* is a vulgarity. It unveils a person, only crudely conscious of what he utters, who has no more respect for the language than he does for his listeners.

like No solecism is as ubiquitous as this one.

• If you are a Wings fan, you have to hope your team plays just *like* it did for most of Monday night's game.
• Jim hopes that Kennedy will beat the odds *like* he has.
• The railroads will be the salvation of this country *like* they were during WWII.
• Our operating system isn't working *like* it should.

Though to the misguided masses, the cachet of using *like* instead of *as* may be appealing, to others it is nothing less than appalling. Knowing when to use *as* instead of *like* is the mark of conscientious people who still value one of the hallmarks of being human: using the language well.

loan *Loan* is a noun. *Lend* is a verb. Today, *loan* is also used as a verb because banks and mortgage companies are concerned with making loans, and the verb *loan,* better than the more casual-sounding *lend,* reminds people that they owe money. Use *lend;* usurers *loan.*

loathe *Loathe* (LOATHE) a verb, means to dislike greatly, hate, or detest; *loath* (LOTH), an adjective, means disinclined, reluctant. If people could grasp the difference in pronunciation, perhaps they could grasp the difference in meaning. Here, too, dictionary makers insult us by suggesting the same pronunciation (and, some, even the same spelling) for both words.

lowest common denominator For some — copycat journalists, delicate marketing people, and feeble-minded social scientists perhaps — *lowest common denominator* is a long-winded, short-sighted way of avoiding more telling words like *worst, nadir, masses, readily accessible:*

- Instead of disseminating the best in our culture, television too often panders to the *lowest common denominator.*
- If you fear making anyone mad, then you ultimately probe for the *lowest common denominator* of human achievement.
- In that environment, each show tried to appeal to the *lowest common denominator.*
- The J.D. InterPrizes' *lowest common denominator* design concept allows for the widest possible viewing audience.

(you) made my day   Often a response to being complimented, *you made my day* appeals to the mass of people who rely on others for their opinion of themselves. And if they embrace others' approval, so they bow to their criticism.

mantel   Some dictionaries maintain that *mantel* is a variant spelling of *mantle,* and *mantle* of *mantel,* but this is hardly helpful. Let the distinct spelling of each word denote the distinct meaning of each word.

marrage The word *marriage* contains i-a-g-e, "I age" — a suitable mnemonic.

masterful *Masterful* means domineering or imperious, whereas *masterly* means skillful or expert. This is another distinction that lexicographers have forsaken. Dictionaries that offer one word as the equivalent of the other, *masterful* as *masterly,* do not enhance our understanding. In fact, the case can plainly be made that dictionary makers — as much as anyone and perhaps more than most — mangle the language by encouraging the erosion of meaning.

meritous *Meritous,* of course, is not a word. At best, it's a mumbler's way of pronouncing *meritorious.*

message In the sense of "to send a message," the verb *message* is disagreeable; in the sense of "to mail, email, write, or tell," it is abhorrent.

metric Among the self-important and the empty-headed, *metric* is displacing *measure* (or *measurement*). No highly regarded dictionary can claim that *metric* is a synonym for *measure,* but as people mimic the best of each other so they mimic the worst.

minutia *Minute* (my-NOOT), an adjective, means exceptionally small; insignificant; extremely thorough and meticulous. *Minutia,* a noun, is a small, trivial detail. Perhaps more disturbing than the misuse of *minutia* for *minute* is the mispronunciation of it. *Minutia* is better pronounced (mi-NOO-shee-ah), not (mi-NOO-sha), as the lazy ones would have it. The plural of *minutia* is *minutiae,* whose only pronunciation is (mi-NOO-shee-ee). Though people may mean *minutiae* (mi-NOO-shee-ee), they invariably spell it *minutia* and pronounce it (mi-NOO-sha).

misconfusion *Confusion, mistake, misunderstanding* are all perfectly good words; *misconfusion* is a word only among those prone to confusion, making mistakes, and misunderstanding.

morays The word for the customs, conventions, or traditions of a community or society is *mores,* not *morays.* People who misspell the word *morays* reveal they do not read, or if they read, they do not think. *Mores* is pronounced MOR-az, not MOR or MORS, despite the second pronunciation that some dictionaries, and others who have no notion of the word, offer. The singular of *mores* is *mos,* pronounced MO.

most (very) definitely It is irredeemably dimwitted to say *most definitely* when the more moderate, indeed, the more civilized *certainly, I (am), indeed; just so, quite right, surely, that's right,* or *yes* will do.

(a) must (miss) Like all badly made terms, *(a) must (miss)* is no sooner said than it sounds stale, no sooner read than it sours. In all its variations — *a must have, a must read, a must see,* and so on — this phrase is altogether too *musty.*

niggardly *Niggardly* (used as an adjective or an adverb) means stingy; parsimonious; meager and inadequate. The noun (or adjective) *niggard,* a miser or stingy person, is seldom seen. Some dictionaries idiotically maintain that *niggardly* (and *niggard*) ought to be used very carefully, if used at all, because many people (no brighter than the average laxicographer) believe that the word means negro (or nigger) and that it is therefore offensive.

nothing could be further from the truth
You would think that anyone who uses this

phrase — anyone, that is, whose words or actions were being questioned or whose honor was being impugned — would choose to speak more eloquently. You would think that unfair or inaccurate accusations would elicit profound and persuasive expressions of denial. When they do not, as they certainly do not when a person resorts to *nothing could be further from the truth,* we have to wonder who is telling the truth and who is not. Formulaic responses like this must make us doubt the sincerity of those who use them.

notoriety *Notoriety* means ill fame, infamy, public humiliation. As a synonym for fame, celebrity, or renown, it is widely misused, especially, it seems, among sportscasters, who may not always think about what they say, and linguists, who never think at all.

obfusticate Some people would have you believe that *obfusticate* (a word doubtless born of mispronunciation) means to darken, becloud, make obscure, confuse, or make unintelligible. Other people know this is the definition of *obfuscate,* truly a word. Proclaiming the validity and usefulness of *obfusticate* is behavior worthy of a half-wit — or a laxicographer.

oblige *Obligate* means to bind or compel by duty or obligation. *Oblige* means to make grateful for a favor or kindness; to do a service or favor for. In decreeing no distinction exists between these two words, lexicographers and linguists would have us all wondering what sense is meant. To lose the distinctions between, the niceties of, words is to strip us of complexity and nuance, of understanding and clarity. Ultimately, any word will do; all words mean all things.

odiferous *Odiferous,* called a variant spelling in some dictionaries, is actually a misspelling of, and incorrect for, *odoriferous.* Very likely, *odiferous* derived from, and endures because of, people's failure to pronounce all five syllables. *Odifrous* (oh-DIF-res) may be next.

on a scale of 1 to 10 The popularity of this phrase is further evidence of the delight some people have with numbers and counting and the distaste they have for words and concepts.

Of course, their fondness for numbers may not go much beyond the count of 10 — so too, perhaps, the number of words in their vocabulary.

on behalf of *On behalf of* means as the agent of; representing. *In behalf of* means in the interest of; for the benefit of. Because most dictionaries ignore the distinction between these two phrases (as they do so many others), people are increasingly ignorant of the distinction; and because people are ignorant of the distinction, ignominy is all. Dictionaries decline thus: ignore, ignorant, ignominy.

on-slot This is what language has come to: meaninglessness. The fierceness of an *onslaught* is wholly lost in childlike spellings such as *on-slot* and *onslot*.

on the same page *On the same page* is spoken or written by pawns and puppets who cannot think for themselves, who rely on others for how they should speak and what they should think, who prize the ease of agreement more than they do the entanglement of dissent, who turn few pages and read fewer books.

on the table There are words that stir, words that persuade, words that compel; *on the table* is not among them.

opinionation Perhaps people who use the regal-sounding, polysyllabic *opinionation* feel as though it gives more weight to their views than does the plainer *opinion.* If laxicographers should ever add *opinionation* to their dictionaries, there will be no reason to consult them further.

or something As there are phrases that help us begin sentences — *I'll tell you (something), Lemme tell you something* — so there are phrases that help us end them. *Or something, or something like that, or something or other* extricate us from having to conclude our thoughts clearly. Said as a person's thoughts end, but before his words do, *or something,* like its many relations, is a thoughtless phrase that reminds us only of our trembling humanity.

past *Passed* is the past tense and past participle of the verb *pass. Past,* a noun, adjective, adverb, or preposition, is never a verb. If this confusion continues, lexicographers and linguists all will sanction it; usage, they maintain, not some notion of correctness or clarity, dictates what's effective.

pay the ultimate price Like other euphemisms, other ludicrous expressions for
death and dying, *pay the ultimate price* —
for be executed; be killed; be murdered; die
— diminishes death, often an avenging,
merciless death. No reverence for the dead,
or for death, is there in this dimwitted expression.

peaceful *Peaceable* means disposed to
peace; promoting calm. *Peaceful* means
undisturbed by strife or turmoil. Almost all
dictionaries now offer *peaceable* as the second definition of *peaceful,* and *peaceful* as
the second definition of *peaceable. Peaceable* is far less often used than *peaceful.*
And *peaceful,* though used in both of the
aforementioned senses, rarely conveys the
principal *peaceable* meaning. With aban-
donment of meaning, there is erosion of
knowledge, less ground for nuance, less soil
for insight.

pedalogical (pedilogical) Dictionaries have
yet to list *pedalogical* (or *pedilogical*) as a
variant spelling of *pedagogical,* but sham
scientists (lexicographers, descriptive linguists, and others equally misguided) will
likely soon begin excusing, justifying, and
promoting these sham spellings.

(as) per (your request) Quintessentially dimwitted, *(as) per (your request)* is used by brainless people who cannot manage to sustain an original thought. These are the people who rely on ready-made phrases and formulas; the people who unquestioningly do as they're told; the people who join mass movements because they themselves cannot bear the burden of making decisions; the people who hate on instruction and fear forever.

permiscuous The people who misspell and mispronounce *promiscuous* seldom have liberal views and values. Descriptive linguists, who generally are liberal thinking, would probably be mortified to mispronounce or misspell this word, but they allow, even encourage, others to do so. Only the small-minded embrace illiberal thoughts and actions, and only the dull-minded embrace ignorance and nonsense.

perspectivize Even more benumbing than *finalize, prioritize,* and *incentivize, perspectivize* finds favor with academicians and others who think their intelligence is most accurately measured by how unintelligible their writing is.

peruse Some dictionaries maintain that *peruse* has two opposite meanings: to read thoroughly and to read hurriedly. *Peruse,* however, means only to read painstakingly, to read carefully, to read thoroughly. It does not mean to glance over or to read quickly. Nor is it a synonym for the word *read.*

pillar of society (the church; the community) It is the *pillars of society* — whether powerful, knowledgeable, or moneyed — who are often the most wobbly among us. Few who have power do not misapply it, few who have knowledge do not misuse it, and few who have money do not misspend it. For these reasons and others, before long and before others, pillars totter and then topple.

poise *Pose,* as a noun, is a bodily position, especially one held for an artist; a way of speaking or behaving. As a verb, *pose* means to adopt a posture; to pretend to be someone else; to be pretentious; to ask a question; to present, especially a problem or threat. *Poise* is ease and grace of manner; composure; self-assurance; a state of equilibrium. As a verb, *poise* means to be balanced or perched. It could very well be that if you lack grace and dignity, if you lack *poise* (POIZ), you spell it p-o-s-e, and pronounce it (POZ).

politeful If *politeful* were a word, it might mean "fulsomely polite." As a synonym for *polite,* it is wholly unnecessary and utterly ridiculous.

• One of our goals is to have the kids grow up to be respectful, courteous, *politeful,* helpful, and loving.
• I am certainly not asking for hand-holding, just a respectful and *politeful* response.
• But he's been very civil, very *politeful;* he's been very respectful of John McCain throughout this whole ordeal.

predominate The adjective is *predominant,* not — despite what some dictionaries now suggest — *predominate. Predominate* is a verb meaning to prevail or dominate. That this word is now sometimes used to mean the adjective *predominant* (having superior strength, authority, influence, or force; most common or conspicuous) is due to people confusing the words and, what's worse, to laxicographers endorsing people's ignorance. The adjective is *predominant.* Writers ought to know that dictionaries chronicle the dissolution of the language;

they are the new doomsday books. Without sensible words, dependable meanings, there can be no sane world.

push the envelope Like many hundreds of English idioms, *push the envelope* helps ensure that any article, any book in which it appears is mediocre and unmemorable. Literature does not allow dimwitted expressions like this; bestsellers demand them.

reach epidemic proportions This phrase and journalistic junk of its kind — for example, *(breathe; heave) a collective sigh of relief; an uphill battle (fight); deal a (crushing; devastating; major; serious) blow to; first (number-one; top) priority; grind to a halt; in the wake of; send a message (signal); shocked (surprised) and saddened (dismayed); weather the storm (of)* — ensure the writers of them will never be seriously read, and the readers of them never thoroughly engaged.

rebound Laxicographers, further disaffecting careful writers and speakers, assign the meaning *rebound* to the definition of *redound.* Of course, it's in the financial interest of dictionary makers to record the least defensible of usages in the English language, for without ever-changing definitions — or as they might say, an evolving language — there would be less need for people to buy later editions of their product.

regimentate To *regiment* means to systematize; to subject to uniformity and order. *Regimentate* is misspelled, mispronounced, misused — just the sort of word that laxicographers long for.

remedy the situation Like all torpid terms, *remedy the situation* neither moves nor motivates us; its use practically ensures that nothing will be righted, nothing remedied. An ill we might be moved to correct, a problem we might be inspired to solve, but a situation we might never be roused to remedy.

replete Ludicrous are the laxicographers who promote *replete* (which means abundantly full) as a synonym for *complete*. Dictionary makers, we must remember, simply document how the language is used; they are not keen thinkers; they do only as they are told.

restless If people continue to watch television more than they read, and listen to music more than they think, and scurry about more than they are silently still, descriptive dictionary makers, who feed on foolishness, will soon claim that *restive* means the same as *restful.*

reticent   *Reticent* means disinclined to speak; taciturn; quiet. *Reluctant* means disinclined to do something; unwilling; loath. Because some people mistakenly use *reticent* to mean *reluctant,* dictionaries now maintain *reticent* does mean *reluctant.* Dictionaries actually promote the misuse of the English language; dictionaries endorse illiteracy.

ripe with   *Ripe* means ready to be harvested; mature; fully grown or developed; pungent or foul smelling. *Rife* means widespread; plentiful. *Rife with* means full of. Infuriatingly, some dictionaries — the worst of them — claim that *ripe with* also means full of. Once we confuse the meanings of words, little is left for us to depend on.

send a (loud) message (signal)   This phrase is a favorite among journalists and politicians — scrawlers and stammerers — who are accustomed to expressing themselves with dead and indifferent words. And from such words, only the faintest of feelings and the shallowest of thoughts can be summoned.

seperate People who do not read or, much the same thing, who read only to be entertained, to be told a story, are likely to spell *separate* s-e-p-e-r-a-t-e. These people do not attend to how words are spelled or sentences fashioned. The tale interests them, not the telling.

sherbert Even though some dictionaries maintain that *sherbert* (SHUR-bert) is acceptable, *sherbet* (SHUR-bit) is the only correct spelling (and pronunciation). This is still another illustration of how lexicographers embrace people's ignorance. Dictionaries have virtually no standards, offer scant guidance, and advance only misunderstanding.

shibboleth Some dictionaries hold that *shibboleth* (SHIB-ah-lith) means a truism; a commonplace saying. But this is simply what people have mistakenly come to believe *shibboleth* means. And dictionaries, ignominiously pandering to the public, record the definition. A *shibboleth* is an identifying word, phrase, custom, or belief that distinguishes a sect, group, or class; a password or watchword.

shocked and saddened Spokespeople and other announcers of platitudes and un-truths use this formula, as well as others very much like it, to express indignation or dismay. But, as a formula, the *shock and sadness* is scarcely heartfelt.

significant other The use of this dispas-sionate expression will likely result in a bloodless relationship with whomever it is used to describe. Any one of the following words is a far better choice: *admirer; beau; beloved; boyfriend (girlfriend); companion; confidant; consort; darling; dear; dearest; familiar; flame; friend; husband (wife); inamorata (inamorato); infatuate; intimate; love; lover; paramour; partner; spouse; steady; suitor; swain; sweetheart.*

The term *significant other* (SO) gives rise to sentiments like this:

Lover: I love you so.
Loved: I love you so, so.

sorely missed Let us not die only to have it said we will be *sorely missed*. We should prefer silence to such insipidity. More disturbing still is that we should be spoken of so blandly, so, indeed, badly. *Sorely missed* is hardly the wording of a tribute, hardly an encomium.

spend *Cost* or *expense, expenditure* or *disbursement* are all infinitely better than the asinine, the asinoun, *spend.* When there is no need to turn a verb into a noun, there can be no patience for it.

• Compared to figures for the first quarter of 2007, the *spend* marks an increase of 50.5 percent.
• The notion essentially provides more options for holidaymakers, and by bringing it to Jamaica, the minister said that it will increase both visitor arrivals and the *spend* of the tourists.
• Today 80% of the *spend* is with 200 suppliers.

staunch *Stanch,* a verb, means to stop the flow of blood or other liquid. *Staunch,* an adjective, means firm, loyal, steadfast; solidly made; substantial. Since so many people confuse one word, or spelling, with the other, dictionaries offer one word as the variant of the other.

straight-laced *Strait-laced* means having strict or severe moral views. (*Strait* is from the Latin *strictus,* strict.) The variant spelling, as descriptive dictionaries label *straight-laced,* is, in truth, a misspelling. The responsibility they had as arbiters of language, dictionaries long ago abnegated. And since they no longer espouse correctness or clarity in language, we obviously can no longer regard them as having much authority in these matters.

superity To eeyores, *superity* is a gloomy collection of letters, too few to mean anything. "Nobody minds. Nobody cares. Pathetic, that's what it is."

(to) take this opportunity (to) On the podium and before others, people speak what they're expected to say. Alone and on their deathbeds, they moan that no one knew who they were. *(To) take this opportunity (to)* is one of the phrases that people learn to mimic before they know to moan.

team player This term is much favored by those in the business world for an employee who thinks just as others do and behaves just as he is expected to. A *team player* is a person who has not the spirit to think for or be himself. Of course, nothing new, nothing innovative is likely to be realized by insisting, as the business world does, on objectivity and consensus.

A *team player* is often no more than a bootlicker; no more than a fawner, a flatterer, a follower; no more than a lackey, a minion, a stooge; no more than a sycophant, a toady, a yes-man.

thank you Even *thank you* — once a sure sign of civility — becomes part of the plebeian patois when it is spoken mechanically.

Only a spectacularly thoughtless person would thank others for having been abused or berated by them, for having been refused or rejected by them.

thank you so much Instead of the genuine-sounding *thank you,* many people are using, almost exclusively, the fulsome-sounding *thank you so much.* That those who use the expression do not understand and cannot hear the artificiality of *thank you so much* is a marvel, and suggests that people do not pay attention to what they or others say. Speech, even the rudimentary words of politeness and civility, is becoming increasingly perfunctory and insincere. And we, increasingly blithe and unaware.

that's how (the way) it goes *That's how (the way) it goes* and other expressions of resignation — of which there are more than a few examples: *such is life; that's how (the way) it goes; that's how (the way) the ball bounces; that's how (the way) the cookie crumbles; that's life; that's life in the big city; that's show biz; what are you going to do; what can you do* — are often spoken by some people and rarely, if at all, spoken by others.

It is obedient, unimaginative — it is dimwitted — people who are too often resigned when they should be complaining, too often resigned when they should be demanding, too often resigned when they should be raging.

that's nice This phrase is used to dismiss what a person has said. *That's nice* is a perfunctory response that, though it suggests interest in a person, actually reveals indifference to the person.

the exception, not (rather than) the rule
Most people find it easier to mimic a repeat-edly used phrase like this — however wordy and inexact, however obtuse and tedious — than to remember a rarely used word like *aberrant* or *anomalous*.

there are no words to describe (express)
There are many more words than people seem to think, and far more is expressible with them than people seem to imagine. Those who depend on dimwitticisms to con-vey thought and feeling are more apt to be-lieve *there are no words to describe,* for these people are, necessarily, most frus-trated by the limits of language.

Dimwitticisms do permit us to describe our most universal feelings, our most banal thoughts, but they prevent us from describ-ing more individual feelings, more brilliant thoughts. These are reserved for a language largely unknown to everyday speakers and writers.

thingify As piteous as the word *thing* usu-ally is, it's not nearly so distasteful as *thingify* (and *thingification*). Though the concept is, in many contexts, repugnant, so, too, is this word used to describe it.

- To use another person is first to *thingify* that person, reduce her to an object, and therefore not to know her as person at all.
- In society's interest of communication, there is consequently a strong tendency to do away with relations by *thingifying* them.
- Once you *thingify* an idea, you find all kinds of behavior that belong with that thing.

tortuous If enough people, in their dull-wittedness, confuse *tortuous* for *torturous,* lexicographers and linguists will call the words synonymic, and berate anyone who tries to keep the distinction alive.

tradegy The misspelling *tradegy* is nothing other than pitiable. Tragedy surrounds us even though social, political, and religious influences try, for their own self-interest not for our sake, to shelter us from much of it. If we can no longer spell the word, it may, in part, be because we scarcely recognize the concept.

transpire *Transpire* means to pass through a surface; to leak out; to come to light; to become known. Unfortunately, its better known meaning — to come about, happen, or occur — is also its worse one, for no other word means quite what the word's less common usage does. The fewer words we know, the fewer thoughts we have.

trepidacious *Trepidacious* (or *trepidatious*) is not a word. Even though people use it (horrible to hear, ridiculous to read though it is), no major dictionary, remarkably, has yet included it in its listing.

up close and personal If we seem to have lost the sense of what it means to be intimate, warm, even romantic, it's partly because vacuous, silly phrases like *up close and personal* have altered our view of meaningful talk and time together.

venerable *Venerable* means worthy of reverence; accorded a great deal of respect. *Vulnerable* means susceptible to attack or injury. Today, when we all seem more vulnerable than ever, and very few people, certainly not our political and corporate leaders, venerable, it may come as little surprise that *venerable* is losing its meaning to *vulnerable*.

versing As a verb form of the preposition *versus* — which we know means against or in contrast with — *versing* is popular among schoolchildren and other intellectual tyros, like descriptive linguists who feel that any word used in any way is a further marvel of language.

viligent *Vigilant* means watchful, alert, attentive. *Viligent* is a solecism, a misspelling. Lexicographers give credibility to solecisms like this by citing misusages; that is, if dictionary makers cared to, they likely could find many instances of *viligent* in writing over the last several centuries. Use alone is often enough for these blackguards to admit a word to their increasingly useless dictionaries.

- Bill Clinton's presidency was rated among the highest for protecting the environment and his wife Hillary will be just as *viligent* in protecting our earth.
- So I'm making a pledge to remain *viligent* on the road to living a more sustainable, peaceful, eco-revering, tree-huggin' lifestyle.
- They usually push me in the directions of throwing everything to the wind instead of being extra-*viligent*.

volumptuous *Voluptuous* means full of, characterized by, or producing delight or pleasure to the senses; suggesting sensual pleasure by fullness and beauty of form; fond of or directed toward the enjoyments of luxury, pleasure, or sensual gratifications. *Volumptuous,* except among lumpen lexicographers, means nothing.

w00t Merriam-Webster, which apparently embraces the idea of being mocked, announced that its 2007 Word of the Year is *w00t* — that's *w*, zero, zero, *t*. It's an alphabetic–numeric word that online gamers use to express their pleasure or approval, their happiness or triumph at, say, having defeated an online enemy. Some people exclaim *yay;* others *w00t.*

Yes, numbers have come to words, owing largely to video games and text messaging, and the dupes at Merriam-Webster who celebrate and promote this idiocy.

Online gamers sometimes substitute letters for numbers to form *l33t* — that's *l*, 3, 3, *t* — or *leet,* speak. *Leet,* short for "elite" — consider the irony — apparently has no more than a handful of words at its disposal, which must be all these "leetle" people need to express their few elementary thoughts.

way The widespread, if witless, use of *way* to mean much or many, far or long, exceedingly or especially reveals how people favor simplicity over precision, easiness over elegance, popularity over individuality. It's unacceptable to use this sense of *way* in your writing, and it's unbecoming in your speaking.

whatever As a one-word response to another's comment or question, *whatever* is as dismissive as it is ill-mannered.

what goes around, comes around This is the secular equivalent of "as you sow, so shall you reap." As such, it is nonetheless a popular prescription, indeed, a moralistic prescription — intoned by those who think in circles — that too easily explains the way of the world.

you do the best you can Dwelling on our failures is no better than dismissing them, but *you do the best you can,* still another expression of resignation, may too easily excuse us for our missteps and mistakes, our failures and inadequacies. Here, *the best* is surely suspect.

you had to be there This is merely an admission of having badly told a tale.

you're joking (kidding) This expression is among the most banal we utter. We say it uncontrollably — less in stupefaction than in stupidity — and without a moment's reflection.

The more commonplace the words you use, the more commonplace the person you are.

3. ODDMENTS AND MISCELLANEA

Responses to Letters

1. My sister and her partner are having an argument over the following: "To piss in your pants" or "To piss your pants." I've seen both but prefer the use of the preposition. What's your verdict?

▶ I hate the word p-i-s-s; not altogether sure why, but I do. But I, too — were I ever to say the phrase — would use the preposition; good personal hygiene demands it.

2. Which spelling should I use, *donuts* or *doughnuts*? (Or, rather, is it all right to use the first — *donuts*?)

▶ *Doughnuts* is the correct spelling, and *donuts*, a variant spelling — a perverted spelling. The people who spell *doughnuts* d-o-n-u-t-s are the people who eat them.

3. Do you favor *email* or *e-mail*? I see both usages, and it seems to me that the former, nonhyphenated usage is more common. To me the hyphenation makes better logical sense, however, since the *e* is not a prefix in the usual sense, but the abbreviation of an entire, long word.

And I know the *New Yorker*, to cite one authoritative publication, still keeps the hyphen.

▶ This is largely a matter of house style. The editors at the *New Yorker* may have decided to use *e-mail*, but *Wired* apparently prefers *email*.

The Chicago Manual of Style, always a few years behind and struggling hopefully for modernity, also recommends *e-mail*. But since they, for years, have recommended that their readers use the spellings found in *Merriam-Webster's Collegiate Dictionary,* I suspect the manual will fall into hopeless desuetude.

I prefer *email* for at least two reasons:

1. *Email* is as understandable as *e-mail;* that is, very few people misunderstand what the nonhyphenated word means or would pronounce it EM-ail.

2. Many compound words evolve from two words to a hyphenated word to a single word: *electronic mail, e-mail, email.* By god, the language does evolve.

I prefer *email* to *e-mail,* and I find no fault with *ebusiness, ebooks,* and *ecommerce.* Yet I may not be so eager to write *eindustry* or *emanufacturing;* here, using the hyphens seems necessary, for without them, the words may not be immediately readable.

Four of the six dictionaries I most often consult list the word as *e-mail* (*email*) — that is, they prefer the hyphenated spelling but allow the nonhyphenated. *Merriam-Webster's Collegiate Dictionary* and *Webster's New World College Dictionary* allow *e-mail* only; neither mentions the spelling *email,* which to my mind, further illustrates how dictionaries are a hotchpotch of inconsistencies and absurdities.

Electronic mail, of course, is not alone in its evolution to becoming one word. Many words have changed similarly. For instance, *lowercase* was initially two words (the bottom or lower drawer in a cabinet that housed the small letters of metal type in a compositor's shop). *Lower case* became *lower-case,* became *lowercase.*

In the computer field, where a wholly unknown term may be widely known within months, we have *data base, data-base, database,* and *on line, on-line, online,* to name but two that have evolved speedily.

4. Which is the correct pronunciation of *short-lived*: is it LIVED with a short-sounding *i* or LIVED with a long-sounding *i*?

▶ Even though most people today pronounce the word with a short *i* sound, and even though most dictionaries offer this pronunciation, the long *i* is correct. The *lived* of *short-lived* derives from the word *life,* not the word *live.*

5. When did *forte* (FOR-tay) become acceptable as a substitute for the proper pronunciation (FORT) in the sense of "someone's strong suit"?

▶ It is not acceptable — despite what your dictionary may tell you. *Forte* (pronounced for-TAY) is a musical instruction meaning loud or forceful. *Forte* (pronounced FORT), one's strong suit; the strongest part of a sword's blade.

Misguided, impressionable people think the words, though spelled the same, are pronounced they same. They are two different words (one of French derivation, one of Italian), and they have two different pronunciations.

6. The following is taken from the NPR Writer's Almanac:

"He was also one of the only generals who loved talking to the press."

Aren't *one* and *only* in contradiction?

▶ Certainly "one of the few" is a better expression. Illogical though "one of the only" is, it's widely used (Google counts more than 650,000 instances of this expression).

Of the six dictionaries I regularly consult, *Merriam-Webster's Collegiate Dictionary,* alone, allows *only* to mean *few.* In fact,

Merriam-Webster's clownlike editors use the expression "one of the only" as their justification for and example of *only* in the sense of *few*.

7. How shall we define *misspeak* in this context:

"Vice President Cheney made perhaps the single most egregious statement about Iraq's nuclear capabilities, claiming: 'we know he has been absolutely devoted to trying to acquire nuclear weapons. And we believe he has, in fact, reconstituted nuclear weapons.' He made this statement just three days before the war. He did not admit until September 14, 2003, that his statement was wrong and that he 'did misspeak.'"

▶ *Lie.* The word *misspeak* is often used, by politicians and others, as a euphemism for "deliberately and willfully lie." The danger here is that the euphemism will become synonymous with the word it is used for. When a word like *misspeak* is used euphemistically for a word like *lie,* we must all loudly complain. Lest euphemisms become synonyms, we must all loudly complain.

People who use *misspeak* in the sense of "lie" know what they mean perfectly well; people not in the habit of lying may not.

8. What is the difference between *special* and *especial*? *The New Yorker* seems to prefer the latter. Is that just an affectation, or is there a real distinction?

▶ Journalists and other writers have forsaken the word *especial,* using *special* almost exclusively. *Special* means particular or specific to someone or something. That *The New Yorker* uses the word *especial* is to be applauded — so long as by it they mean more than special; preeminent; outstanding or exceptional. What's more, to be *special* is hardly a compliment; it may mean you are simply ordinary, or that you are decidedly unordinary. Are we not, today, all drearily *special*? I'd far rather be cranky or foolish or unbearable. And so should you.

9. How and why did the word *fetch* become popular with the U.S. stock market media? Example: "Xerox fetched $10 at today's closing." My third-grade teacher taught us that this word was not acceptable English.

▶ *Fetch,* in the sense of "to go after and bring back," though perfectly good English, may seem informal and folksy to some. It does to me, as perhaps it did to your teacher. The meaning "to sell for a certain price" has no stigma even though the U.S. financial market does.

10. I was wondering if you have any views or information about when the phrase *thinking outside the box* infiltrated the language — and what its origins are.

▶ I don't know the origin of the phrase *thinking outside the box*, but the origin scarcely matters. That people do not tire of this phrase matters, for it has quickly become a hackneyed expression for "be clever, be creative, be inventive, be original, be innovative." People who use this phrase nicely illustrate the antithesis of what it means.

11. I have listened to English professors argue about this question: When you answer the phone, is the correct response "It's me" or "It is I"? (Personally, I get out of the entire dilemma by just saying "Speaking.")

▶ People do argue for both expressions: *It* or *This is me* and *It* or *This is I.* When I answer the phone, I say, *This is he* or, more often, the startlingly correct *I am he.*

Less formal, and not thought incorrect, is using *me* instead of *I* (or *he* or *she*).

The rule, however, is to use a nominative pronoun after some form of the verb *to be,* but as *It's me* and many other expressions make clear, the rule is seldom observed.

12. Even though my dictionary acknowledges both pronunciations of *often* and notwithstanding the fact that "of-ten" is more commonly heard, isn't it preferable to say "of-en"?

▶ OFF-en is the preferred pronunciation even though you may, as frequently, hear people pronouncing it OFF-ten.

OFF-en, of course, requires less effort to articulate than does OFF-ten. In a society that seems to value easiness (and entertainment) over all, it may be surprising that the *t* burst in OFF-ten finds such favor.

With the influence of phonetic spelling and speak as you spell, some people began pronouncing the *t* in *often* — even though they never seemed to have thought to pronounce it in *soften* or *listen* or *hasten*. It is likely that people are less influenced by movements and teachings than they are by one another, by mimicry: people imitate what they hear. There is scant originality of thought, but there is a great deal of doing as others do.

13. Is the preposition *to* required with the use of *oughtn't*? For example, "We oughtn't to think poorly of all lexicographers" vs "We oughtn't think poorly of all lexicographers"? My British editor inserts the preposition; my American editor deletes it. Is it a UK vs US thing? Is one of them dead wrong?

▸ *Ought not,* like *ought* alone, requires *to.* If your American editor recommends your not using *to,* recommend he find a new line of work.

14. "He pet the dog" or "He petted the dog"? The dogs don't mind which way we say it, but my husband and I disagree on which is appropriate. I say, "He bet $5 on the line" makes *me* right. My other half says "He jetted half-way around the world" makes *him* correct.

▶ Though many irregular verbs exist for us to struggle over conjugating, *pet* is not one of them. Further, neither *bet* (which also permits the past tense *betted*) nor *jetted* matters one bit to the past tense of *pet*. Your husband is correct this time: *petted* is the past tense of *pet*. Even Google, not necessarily an arbiter of good usage, agrees: 29 results show "He pet the dog," whereas 110 results show "He petted the dog." All the same, before long, I bet dictionaries (which simply — and, if you ask me, absurdly — compile how people use the language) will show *pet* as an alternative past tense.

15. I thought *scurrilous* meant using foul language, but the only sense I hear the word used these days is exemplified in sentences like this:

"Of course, the Bush campaign's scurrilous lies about Kerry's record as a war hero must be challenged forcefully."

▶ *Scurrilous* (SKUR-ah-les) does mean expressed in, or given to, coarse or vulgar language. But *scurrilous,* which originally meant speaking the language of a buffoon, has taken on still another meaning, which only some dictionaries now recognize: making defamatory claims about someone. My suspicion is that people confuse *scurrilous* with *scandalous,* and thus, today, many dictionaries mindlessly maintain that *scurrilous* is a synonym for making scandalous or defamatory remarks.

There is no need for *scurrilous* to mean scandalous since we have that word and others, but to lose, or be about to lose, *scurrilous* in the sense of expressing coarse language is a shame, for with the loss of that meaning there is increasing, if unspoken, permission to use foul language — about which I complain not for senseless moral reasons but for sound linguistic ones.

16. Is it merely careless pronunciation, or is it an accepted shift in meaning, that accounts for the now common use of *tenant* in place of *tenet*?

▶ It's careless pronunciation, careless spelling, careless reading, careless thinking, all of them the ingredients of and the truth behind modern-day dictionary making. No dictionary that I am aware of holds that *tenant* means *tenet,* but every one of them soon will if people do not use the language carefully. As democracy falters when we neglect it, so does language fail.

17. Why has the phrase *gone missing,* a primarily British expression to the best of my knowledge, crept into the American mediaspeak? It's as if missing is a destination or a recreational activity, like fishing or shopping.

▶ People are so dull-witted and impressionable that, today, in this country, the popularity of *gone* or *went missing* has soared. Words like *disappeared, vanished, misplaced, stolen, lost, deserted, absconded* are seldom heard today because *went missing* has less meaning, or less exact meaning, than any of them, and people, especially the media, perhaps, are afraid of expressing meaning. What's more, *went missing* sounds willful or deliberate, and, indeed, sometimes that connotation is accurate, but the child who has been kidnapped is hardly agreeable to having been so.

Went missing appeals to people because it's largely meaningless and because it's a fad term. Few people who are conscious of how they speak, of the words they use, say *gone* or *went missing.*

18. Has the use of *whom* been abandoned? Iunderstand that in normal conversation it may be difficult to quickly choose the correct form, *who* or *whom,* but not when writing. A *Daily News* headline read "Who Shot Who?" Any comment?

▶ "She Shot He?" Only presidents and their kind talk this way, ignoring all distinction between nominative and objective pronouns. *Whom* is an objective pronoun, comparable to *me, him, her, them, us,* and thus demands the linguistic respect it is entitled to, meaning it ought to be correctly used.

Showing respect for the word is not enough; let's also deny it to those who would say, or, even more reprehensible, write, a sentence like "Who Shot Who?"

Knowing when to use *whom* is more than most people can manage. And if people rarely use *whom* in spoken English, they quickly become disinclined to use it in written English. Clumsy speech influences us more than careful writing does.

If we know when to use *me* or *him* or *her* or *them* or *us,* then we know — or we ought to know — when to use *whom.* Of course, many people do not know when to use these objective case pronouns.

If *whom* sounds "stilted" in spoken English, it's surely because we seldom hear it used. People have been prognosticating about the disappearance, the death of the word *whom* for some years, but it endures, here and there, among those who still value elegance in language.

19. I thought I would ask what you think of "10 items or less." Bill Walsh, a copy editor at the *Washington Post* and until now a reasonable guy, has caved and accepts it.

▶ The distinction between *fewer* and *less* (like that between *number* and *amount*) centers on what can be counted and what cannot. *Fewer* we use for numbers; *less* we use for quantities. But, here, too, some of our worst dictionaries maintain that *less* is synonymous with *fewer,* and *fewer* with *less.* It is not time to acquiesce, as Walsh apparently has done; it's time we all loudly complain.

20. What's your take on *The New Yorker*'s use of the diaeresis? I'm no expert, but *reelection* with an umlaut on the second *e* looks odd to me.

▶ It looks no more odd than it is. The dieresis, which is rarely used today (though occasionally in *naïve*), is placed atop the second of two juxtaposed vowels to indicate two separate sounds are to be pronounced. And though two sounds are found at the beginning of *reelection*, no one (except perhaps the U.S. president seeking reelection, the lexicographers at Merriam-Webster's, and the editorial staff at *The New Yorker*) is likely to pronounce the word ree-LEK-shen.

The hyphen, far more often than the dieresis, is used in this country to indicate two sounds, but more often still to separate a prefix from a word stem or to distinguish one word from another (*re-create* from *recreate,* for instance).

Other Remarks

1. "Every single moment of your life you are faced with a choice irregardless of your station in life, irregardless of your status, irregardless of your circumstances or your limitations." — Diana Rogers, Crystal Clear Reflections

► *Irregardless* is nonstandard used once, illiterate used twice, barbarous three times.

2. "More recently the concept of humanism has been incorporated into the tenants of Unitarian Universalism, which is practiced by over 160,000 people in the U.S. alone, and many more globally." — Cynthia D. Trombley, *Observer-Tribune*

► Neither Trombley nor her editor seems to know the meaning of *tenant.* What other words do they not know? What other words do they confuse the meanings of? What thoughts do they not think because they do not know the words to think them with? And of the thoughts they can think, how many are muddled or mistaken because they confuse the words they use to think them?

3. "My distracting point with drugs was during my second year in the faculty of commerce and by the second term I was constantly injecting myself with cocaine and occasionally sniffing heroine." — Reham Wafy, Teen Stuff Online

► That ending *e* makes quite a difference. All who believe that meaning matters little, that spelling matters less, that usage matters least, consider our fair *heroin.*

4. "SuperMat clean is a clean you can see. ... SuperMat clean is a clean you can feel. ... SuperMat clean is a clean you can hear." — Kleen-Tex Industries

▶ KleenTex is a company you can tease. ... KleenTex is a company you can mock. ... KleenTex is a company you can scorn.

5. "The Office on Aging, which falls under the auspicious of the Department of Human Services, seeks to help improve the quality of lives of our senior citizen population." — Department of Human Services, Perth Amboy, New Jersey

▶ On the other hand, it could be that the Office on Aging encourages the mental deterioration of its elderly population by confusing them with expressions like *under the auspicious of.*

6. "We can no longer quote fares or respond by email; our posted addresses are being unindated by spam, viruses, worms, and forwarding via address spoofs." — Los Angeles Yellow Cab

▶ We sympathize with Yellow Cab's plight, but not with its inuntelligent use of unindated.

7. "If I would have been a publishing house, I would've eagerly taken David's book." — Rich Lowry, Editor, *National Review*

▶ Mr. Lowry's use of *would have* (instead of *had*) exposes an inability to reason well — as does his imagining he might conceivably have been a publishing house.

8. "A quick, easy customer experience garnered Yahoo the success it enjoys today — and the new prominence of Yahoo Shopping complexifies the experience and could threaten Yahoo's core experience." — Creative Good Inc.

▶ *Complexifies?* The author either is unfamiliar with the word *complicates* or does not know the difference between neologism and nonsense.

9. "They're still a very good person who made a tremendous mistake and a misjudgment." — Reverend Jerome F. Gillespie

▶ From our religious leaders, we should expect an understanding of pronoun–antecedent agreement, if not of human nature.

10. "This site has a great deal of information about the basics of English grammer."
— Mid-Continent Public Library

▶ The basics of English *grammar* surely include knowing how to spell the word.

11. "The purpose of language is to communicate, rather than prescribe to rules and standards. ... Moreso, though, rules were either created or sternly upheld by those insecure, upper-class intellectuals who insisted upon them to prove their education over of that of the lower elements." — Scott Kapel, *Solecisms of Mechanics and Grammar*

▶ The correct word is *subscribe,* not *prescribe,* though I suspect the author of this sentence, an English teacher and a so-called descriptive grammarian, might try to rebut this. Moreover, as any of his students might conceivably tell him, *moreso* is not a word. Both of Kapel's sentences show as little sense of grammar as they do of reason.

12. "The findings demonstrate that children disprefer learning a different, unrelated meaning for a known word when that word is used in a linguistic context that fails to bias strongly for a new meaning." — Devin Casenhiser, Department of Linguistics, University of Illinois

▶ This one sentence, scarcely intelligible as it is, should dissuade all of us from having much faith in linguists and their pronouncements. If linguists want to use a word like *disprefer,* let them first learn how to write a readable sentence.

13. "Anyway, his tragic passing got me thinking a lot about death and how permanent the condition is. You can never go back. It's an awesome concept if you really think about it." — Lisa Klugman, Editor in Chief, *Fit*

▶ This is the writing of a fifth grader, for whom, it's not bad, but for an editor of a national magazine, it's execrable. Not only for its style but also for its sensibility is it atrocious, for it has neither.

14. "Dominique's double life began unraveling last year, when the 50-year-old doctor was killed in a hit-and-run accident." — Verena Dobnik, Associated Press

▶ Writers surely read a good deal: articles, essays, short stories, novels, poetry — almost anything but what they themselves write.

15. "And the enormity of the honor that you have bestowed upon him is still sinking in." — Lynne Cheney, wife of U.S. vice president Dick Cheney

▶ Enough of this misusage. *Enormity* is a word like no other; let us not disembowel it by using it as a synonym for *enormousness,* which of course, is sated with synonyms.

16. "After graduating high school in 1985, Kravits received an acting scholarship to the University of Maryland and spent the next six years doing theater in Washington, D.C., before moving to New York City, where he acted in commercials and small theater productions." — Jason Lynch and Allison Singh Gee, *People*

▶ Two people are apparently not enough to write a grammatically correct sentence at *People* magazine, where the writing is so often reminiscent of someone who never did graduate *from* high school.

17. "These attacks are only the tip of the iceberg. They are the part of the iceberg that is visible above the water — in clear view. But as everyone knows, the largest part of the iceberg, and possibly the most dangerous, lies beneath the surface of the water and is difficult to detect." — U.S. Senator Bob Bennett

▶ Not only are we subjected to the monstrous and omnipresent *tip of the iceberg image,* but this U.S. senator feels as though he needs to explain what he means by it. From our senators, we should expect eloquence, not inanity.

18. "When the organizers were able to alleve her of her concerns, the concert was back on again." — Lola Ogunnaike, CNN

▶ Ogunnaike and others who use the absurdity *alleve* ought to be dismissed from their jobs for apparent pill-popping.

19. "Annie Dillard says in her *The Writing Life,* 'The writing life is colorless to the point of sensory depravation.'" — Philip Yancy, as quoted in ChristianityToday.com

▶ If we believe Dillard wrote *deprivation* and Yancy said *deprivation,* we must wonder at how deprived of depravity, or old-fashioned fun, perhaps, the good people at Christianity Today are.

20. "I called my mom, I go, 'Did you read this?' She goes, 'Un-hunh.' And I go, 'You didn't say anything?' And she goes, 'No, I'm sure he deserves it,' with a nice bit of sarcasm. I go, 'Well, I didn't, don't worry.'" — David Spade, actor

▶ Only the adolescent or the addlebrained prefer *go* or *went* to *say* or *said* or other words.

21. "The affair caused rifts within families. People fought duals over it. There was talk of civil war." — NPR Writer's Almanac

▶ A compelling account of the Dreyfus Affair, a story of courageous behavior by some and despicable behavior by others, has as its denouement, a mistake that unsettles every reader more attentive than the writer.

22. "Wear as the Canadians have repeatedly booed the American National Anthem at sporting events in Vancouver, Toronto and Montreal and government officials have repeatedly insulted the great President of the United States and impugned the integrity of the of its people." — Gregg Henson, Boycott Canada

▶ Not only does Mr. Henson not know what a sentence is, he doesn't know what a word is, and least of all does he know what reason is. People who do not write well are people who do not think well.

Imprecation

Liber scriptus proferetur —
dictionaries have had their day
in quo totum continetur —
dictionaries have had their day
unde mundus judicetur —
dictionaries have had their day
Dies irae, dies irae, dies irae

Imprecation

Accursed one who lies, who sneaks, who
cheats

With big-bellied words, droopy-sentence
  teats.
Our blood's been bled, our hearts no longer
  stir.
Your words will always chill us, *br, brr,
  brrr.*

A Little Chat with Members of the American Dialect Society Listserv

In a message dated 6/17/2003 4:50:35 PM
Eastern Daylight Time, pulliam@iit.edu
writes:

I also think that many people feel very
threatened by language change and varia-
tion. You can see this in the TVR's motto [A
society is generally as lax as its language],
which appears to be based on a real, if un-
founded and therefore illogical, fear that the
language changes taking place around us
are some sort of vanguard of social and cul-
tural change — for the worse.

Robert Hartwell Fiske wrote:

I am not the least fearful of language
change though I am fearful of ignorance,
and only the honest among you will concur

that much language change is due to exactly that.

I imagine, though, that the principal reason for the vituperative (and ad hominem) attacks against me is that people who have spent their lives studying linguistics are infuriated when someone dares say, in effect, that how they see things is largely nonsense. No one likes to be told, even implicitly, that he has wasted his life.

In a message dated 6/18/2003 12:56:31 PM Eastern Daylight Time, gordonmj@missouri.edu writes:

Given the contempt Fiske has for linguists, it's interesting that he proudly lists the mysterious ADS "endorsement" of Vocabula [The Vocabula Review is an excellent regular publication ... digestible by the academic and layman alike. — American Dialect Society] on his site among other comments praising the publication.

In a message dated 6/19/2003 8:17:56 AM Eastern Daylight Time, gbarrett@world-newyork.org writes:

I'm sure I looked at the Vocabula Review site for ten minutes three years ago, found it inoffensive, and whipped off a few lines to cover the link. I couldn't tell you why I even bothered with a review. I'm no Michiko Kakutani. I've looked at the VR site a few times since and have usually felt the articles I had access to stopped about ten thousand words short of explaining the true mission of their subtext. So, since I added the link, I have come to concur with the general opinion on the Vocabula Review.

Robert Hartwell Fiske wrote:

Now that Barrett has decided that the Vocabula site is as objectionable as others here have maintained, I, too, will remove the ADS endorsement that he wrote some years ago.

Apparently, descriptivists are hell-bent to unearth "subtexts"; prescriptivists wish only to write well and clearly. Any subtext in Vocabula articles is of Barrett's imagining; what's more, I dare say, he has not read any of Vocabula's articles in at least a year; he does not subscribe, and he does not know of what he speaks.

Truly I had no contempt for linguists (though I didn't much care, as I made plain, for the tone of the attacks against me), but I'm now understanding that linguists (very well, some linguists) are lemming-like. However would you manage if the country were overcome by terrorists or North Koreans or evangelical conservatives? Tergiversate? Become quislings? A society *is* generally as lax as its language.

As I believe I have said before, only a handful of ADS members do subscribe to The Vocabula Review. The rest of you (who have participated in railing against me and Vocabula) have not read TVR, but you have felt you can judge it harshly (based, I suppose, on a four-paragraph mission statement — which by the way, I wrote some years ago; TVR has evolved over time even if the mission statement has not). This is surely the antithesis of liberalism.

The final point I wish to make is that I welcome alternative or opposing views in Vocabula; descriptivists have written articles for Vocabula. ADS, it must now be clear, does not tolerate free-thinking any more than it does a prescriptivist approach.

fiske *v.* 1. to rail against dull-witted lexi-cographers and descriptive linguists. 2. to point out unconscionable stupidity. 3. to battle mercilessly and relentlessly; to at-tack. 4. to be criticized by Robert Hartwell Fiske.

• He fiskes Merriam-Webster with his monthly "Mock Merriam" column.
• They've been fisked.
• His physique is as fearsome as his fisking.

Vocabula Polls

1. The misspelling and mispronunciation of *odoriferous* stinks.

The misspelling and mispronunciation *odif-erous* stinks, yes.   86%

Apparently, *odiferous* was first recorded in the 15th century. Can it be frowned upon in the 21st century?   14%

Odiferous is easier to pronounce than *odor-iferous*. The fewer syllables a word has the better.   0%

2. I love the word *def.* Slang is sexy, and so am I.

I'm wid-ja, bro. *Def* is phat. 11%

Most definitely does *def* add to the language. 33%

Def's days are numbered. 11%

Def is an absurd word that appeals only to idiots and laxicographers. Keep mocking Merriam! 44%

3. *W00t* should be included in the next, the twelfth, edition of Merriam-Webster's.

If it is, I'll burn my copy. 52%

Good Lord, I hope not. 20%

Sure, why not? 20%

W00t, w00t! 8%

4. Using *alright* instead of *all right* is:

harmless: 34%

silly: 2%

idiotic: 5%

illiterate: 47%

harmful: 13%

5. People who have a prescriptive attitude toward language must be politically and socially conservative.

Yes, how we use the language should be ineluctably associated with our moral purpose and perspective. 8%

It's the people who mix affiliations — the prescriptive liberals, the descriptive conservatives — who are befuddled; they know not who they are. 5%

Political and social views do not necessarily mean anything in relation to language. You can be a liberal Democrat and a prescriptivist, as you can be a conservative Republican and a descriptivist. 77%

What? People have attitudes toward language? 9%

6. New Year's Resolutions

I resolve to scold anyone, publicly if possible, who speaks solecistically and writes wretchedly. 7%

I will redouble my efforts to speak and write clear, correct English. 59%

I will go where the language takes me; complaining about none of it, delighted by all of it. 24%

Resolution-schmesolution. I will speak English as well or as badly as I have all these years. 9%

I resolve to let the poorly educated, the laxicographers, the insensate help me decide how to speak and write the language. 2%

7. A person who does not speak well is a person who does not think well.

Quite so, consider the often blithering president of the United States. 27%

This equation is more true than not. 15%

We certainly do better when thinking precedes speaking. 38%

How you speak has no bearing on how you think. 9%

Not so, consider the mind-numbing prescriptivists at Vocabula. 11%

8. The new slang-filled 11th edition of the *Merriam-Webster Collegiate Dictionary* does as much as, if not more than, *Webster's Third* to discourage people from taking lexicographers seriously.

This dictionary includes words like "funplex," "McJob," "headbanger," "Frankenfood," "phat," and "dead presidents." Laughable words compose this laughable book. 17%

Almost all slang, the people at Merriam-Webster should know, is ephemeral. Most of the slang added to the 11th edition will likely never see the 12th. 32%

Anyone who speaks of "dead presidents" probably will be hired for nothing other than a "McJob." 11%

These slang terms have currency; they define the times and belong in the new Merriam-Webster. 33%

Rich and inventive terms testify to the vitality of our language. We should embrace these terms and use them unreservedly. 7%

9. More than incorrect grammar and an infelicitous style, the deliberate misuse of words — euphemism, circumlocution, lying — is an assault on language and society.

Yes, of course. Enron, Merrill Lynch, and others are despicable corporate citizens. Unrelenting, impenitent liars. Consider the people who have suffered owing to their behavior. 51%

Perhaps. Bush and his minions have likely known all along that there are no weapons of mass destruction in Iraq. And despite the deaths, despite the lies, are we or the Iraqis thus worse off? 22%

Unlikely. Lying is part of the mix of language and behavior. Nothing much could be achieved without the rhetoric of lies. 15%

Not so. Lies and evasion are inherent in language. Without them, there is no language. 12%

10. Dictionaries should be much more pre-scriptive, far less descriptive, than they now are.

Yes! More than that, laxicographers pro-mote the dissolution of the English lan-guage (and even society) with their misguided liberality. 26%

Quite so. Dictionary compilers need to maintain, and perhaps even decide, distinc-tions between words; they need to guide us on matters of usage. 36%

A mix of guidance and license is probably the best course — it's also the commonest course. 28%

Lexicographers are necessarily descriptivist for their job is simply to record how people use the language. 11%

Obviously, we all must bow to the defini-tions and spellings found in the dictionary. 0%

11. Let's stop adulating sports figures, rock stars, and other celebrities. A person who can declaim, who can speak beautifully, is truly someone to prize.

Hear, hear. I thoroughly agree. People who can speak well and honestly would make worthy, and uncommon, heroes. 52%

Can we not have both? 48%

You're a crackpot. Sports figures, rock stars, movie personalities are far more valuable than someone who can speak a clear sentence. 0%

12. A society is generally as lax as its language.

An axiom; there can be little doubt of this. 22%

Yes, I imagine there is some truth to this. 41%

I don't know. How is one to know? 16%

No, I doubt whether there is much truth to this. 9%

A preposterous and unsubstantiated thought. 11%

The boneman cometh.